To

for your future

Never lose yourself.

Claire

x

EDGE! A Leadership Story

By Bea Fields and Corey Blake with Eva Silva Travers

EDGE! A Leadership Story

By Bea Fields and Corey Blake with Eva Silva Travers

ISBN: 978-0-9814545-4-2 Paperback
ISBN: 978-0-9814545-3-5 Hardcover
Library of Congress Control Number: 2008924507

Published By:

1117 Windbrooke Drive, Suite 202
Buffalo Grove, IL 60089
Phone: 847.682.3493
press.writersoftheroundtable.com

Cover Design and Interior Layout by:
Nathan Brown
Writers of the Round Table Inc

Table of Contents

FOREWORD By Micheal E. Gerber
ACKNOWLEDGMENTS

Chapter ONE: Unrest 11

Chapter TWO: Disclosure 19

Chapter THREE: Reality Check 26

Chapter FOUR: Rejected 33

Chapter FIVE: Alone 50

Chapter SIX: Epiphany 63

Chapter SEVEN: Provocation 71

Chapter EIGHT: Fear 87

Chapter NINE: Avoidance 97

Chapter TEN: Digging 104

Chapter ELEVEN: Feedback 117

Chapter TWELVE: Vulnerability 143

Chapter THIRTEEN: Truth 155

Chapter FOURTEEN: Authenticity 168

Chapter FIFTEEN: Blindsided 174

Chapter SIXTEEN: Doubt 179

Chapter SEVENTEEN: Running 189

Chapter EIGHTEEN: Devastation 194

Chapter NINETEEN: Breathing 199

Chapter TWENTY: Taking Command 207

Chapter TWENTY ONE: Redesigning 224

Chapter TWENTY TWO: Standing Up 237

Foreword

I have admitted to this before, but I think it's important to say it again: I don't *read* business books, I *write* them. On the other hand, I'm often asked by friends, peers, and fans to "take a look" at their manuscript and say a word or two about how significant their book is and why I think it's a must read for you. I absolutely hate when that happens! Primarily, because I know that I will not like what I read, and then I'll be forced to alienate a friend, defrock a peer, and forever lose a fan. What to do, what to do?

So, when my friend Corey Blake and his co authors of *Edge*, Bea Fields and Eva Silva, came to me with the verboten request to "take a look at their book" I felt that same sense of dread I always feel under those circumstances. And, as I almost always do because I cannot bring myself to say no, I said okay, and then avoided the inevitable for more than two months, trying to find a reason why my schedule would make it *impossible* for me to do what I had promised to do.

When Corey called again I found myself in the impossible position of having to do what I said I would do. So, I bit my lip, took a long drink, and sat down and began to read.

You should read this book, too!

This is a tale of a man who doesn't know how to lead, but is one, like so many leaders you and I have met.

This is a business tale about the conflict between the man that needs to lead and the one who doesn't know how to that brings itself to bear, not only on the man himself, but on everyone he comes into contact with. In *Edge*, we get to understand what being on the leadership edge means, not in moralistic terms, but internally to the one experiencing it, and externally on those living with the one who is experiencing it upon whose decisions each and every player in the system grows to depend.

Even more important, *Edge* is not a business book per se, but a book about leadership, the role everyone in a role of authority must learn to play. If she or he does, magic happens. If he or she doesn't, the opposite accrues: people are hurt, objectives go most often unfulfilled, energy goes wasted, and that deadening feeling of time lost and never to be regained becomes an overriding feeling of despair as decisions are made.

How this transformation happens in *Edge* is what most inspired me. Our hero comes face to face with a coach.

But not just any coach. In *Edge*, our coach is someone I wish I knew when I needed one. She is a dazzler. (At least she dazzled me!) She possesses the wisdom of someone who knows there's no time to waste working with foolish people. She's direct, has a sureness about her, asks questions I knew I should answer, and in the end achieves what she set out to do, with such deftness and deliberate coolness, I wondered how Corey, Bea and Eva made her up (Only after reading the book did I find out that the coach was based on author and leadership coach, Bea Fields...Bravo!).

And that's the wonder of *Edge*. I left it with more of an edge than I had when I picked it up.

I won't tell you the surprise ending because there isn't one. There's just a remarkable process that a wonderful book always takes me through.

All I can say is: Thank you, Corey. Thank you, Bea. And, thank you, Eva. Thank you for *Edge*.

You came through!

Michael E. Gerber
Author of the E-Myth books
Chief Dreamer of In The Dreaming Room

Acknowledgments and Thanks from Bea Fields

There are so many people to thank, mainly:

My husband Mike Fields for his constant encouragement and support for my business and in helping to manage my day in day out business operations.

My three amazing kids, Ann, Katie and Jack Fields for keeping me laughing and always sharp and on my toes.

My parents, Anise and Turk Roberts for their love and for encouraging me to use my talents to their fullest.

My sisters, Edie Smith and Terry Duke, for being there for me any time of the day or night.

Windy and Mike Pratt for helping me get my coaching business off the ground and up and running in less than three months. Thank-you Windy and Mike!

My mentor coaches: Karen Whitworth, Duncan Coppock, Dave Buck and Tom Shields who have helped me become a confident, no-nonsense executive coach.

My coach, Sue McLeod, for truly standing for me to turn this idea of a book into a reality. Her coaching helped me understand that I have a unique message to share with the world.

To the following people who taught me how to be successful in the business aspects of operating a coaching practice: Alicia Smith, Michael Port, Kimberly George, Mitch Meyerson, Dave Buck, Thomas Leonard, Dale Noles, Cliff Walker, and Raluca Ciuperca.

To the entire staff of Coach University, CoachVille and the Georgetown University Coaching Program for training me with such exceptional standards. I could not have written this book without the education you offer to aspiring coaches.

To Corey Blake, Eva Silva Travers, Sue Publicover and David Charles Cohen and the entire Writers of the Round Table team for partnering with me to turn this creative idea into a manuscript. Knowing you has truly changed my life.

ONE | Unrest

Mitchell James, CEO of Global Trade Management, ran quickly through the front door of the office building, shaking off his umbrella and cursing the recent burning in his stomach. He hated DC winters. Even more, he hated the Wall Street Journal tucked under his arm that made a fresh mockery of Global's stocks and the account they'd just lost to their arch competitor—not to mention the loss of their top salesman who abandoned them with the account. There it was in black and white for the world to see. Eating away at him were two thoughts: the steady fall of revenues and the consistent departure of key team players during his time as CEO. As the security guard at the entrance to the building said good morning, Mitch reminded himself that most people *liked* him, or seemed to any way. So why weren't they sticking around?

Pouring himself a cup of coffee from freshly ground beans, Mitch closed his eyes and breathed in the aroma. He turned to grab a handful of raw almonds from the cupboard. "Morning, Maxy," he said, moving his glasses to the top of his head.

"Morning, Mitch," she said, with a sideways glance.

Silence ensued over the next twenty seconds while she poured a cup of black coffee into her own ceramic mug and then turned to leave. As Mitch turned to watch her walk away, she flipped her hair and merely nodded at Stephen, the company's Corporate Financial Officer, before she continued through the door. Characteristically clad in a custom tailored broad-shouldered, narrow-waisted suit, Stephen turned his chiseled physique sideways, letting Maxy pass while giving her the once over. Clearing his throat, Mitch turned to close the cupboard as nonchalantly as possible. Sensing an opening, Stephen finally moved his eyes from Maxy's backside to Mitch with a predictably sly grimace.

"Ah, yes...I sense the end of an era," Stephen said, running a hand over his thick, dark brown hair.

Mitch always felt himself on the verge of telling Stephen that his hair made him look like John Travolta in *Saturday Night Fever*, but felt it best to avoid conversation whenever possible, as the very sound of Stephen's voice had grown to grate on his nerves. "What do you mean?" Mitch said, recognizing and regretting the defensive tone in his voice.

"Aw, c'mon, Mitchell. We can all see it. She's one of the best at what she does....but she's bored. Restless. How many times a day does she come for coffee these past few weeks. Nah..." he continued, making a shot of espresso, "you can't keep a woman like that in your *bedroom* for long, let alone your *boardroom*."

Mitch bit his lip, searching for something to say that wouldn't make him sound like a 20-year old and looked up at the dry-erase calendar board on the wall. The left side was filled top to bottom with meeting dates for prospective accounts and the right side was filled with an agenda for the upcoming executive team meeting. Much to Mitch's chagrin, along the bottom was someone's anonymous stab: "Another one bites the dust! So long, Mira from accounting!" He had to look away.

Regaining his composure a bit, Mitch quickly changed the subject. He pulled his glasses back down over his eyes and said matter-of-factly, "Well, speaking of the boardroom, I need your preliminary quarterly on my desk by Friday." *End of conversation*, Mitch thought to himself as he walked directly to his office, knowing full well that it was not, in fact, the end. He had merely pried open his own can of worms just a little further. Maxy *was* restless. The numbers reflected in the quarterly report would be less than acceptable, just as they'd been the previous two quarters. Worse than *those* cold hard facts was the fact that he didn't know what the hell to do about either situation.

At his mahogany desk, he drew a deep breath that seemed somewhat ragged to him and crossed one ankle over the opposite knee. He picked up his favorite Cross pen without thinking about it and started tapping out a tune. His left hand became a conduit for the current soundtrack that was running through his subconscious mind—2001, A *Space Odyssey*. In particular, the opening sequence of Richard Strauss's *Thus Sprach Zarathustra* had been repeating itself in his head for days; his wife, Anna, had finally watched it with him Sunday night.

Suddenly, the buzz of the intercom brought him back to reality. Clearing his throat and sitting up a little straighter, Mitch answered the call. He was relieved that it was Graham's voice on the other end.

Mitch considered the ever vibrant but serene Graham more of a confidant than he'd ever actually admit. As the current Vice President of Sales, Graham had quickly risen through the salesperson-ranks since joining Global Trade Management Corporation. As stellar as his resume was, Mitch found his demeanor even more persuasive and endearing; he seemed more like an older brother or someone he wished had been his neighborhood friend as a kid, though Mitch imagined Graham's tastes had probably always run along eclectic lines and would have intimidated him back in the day.

"Hey, Boss Man! It's your friendly neighborhood town-crier!"

Mitch smiled. He always expected this kind of greeting.

"How goes it?"

"Great, great. I'm just getting together the numbers for the team meeting." Mitch answered, waiting uneasily for whatever news his informant had to share.

"Ah, yes, the all-important numbers," Graham said in a softer, lilting, almost condescending tone.

Mitch always felt that Graham's comments like these, though slight in sarcasm, were intended as the opening line for some lesson his friend never completed, like a fortune cookie with no fortune inside.

"So what's the news today, oh Great Herald Down the Hall?"

"Patience, Grasshopper," Graham said in a mock Chinese accent. "The road to enlightenment comes only with a promise to join me for lunch today. Agreed?"

Mitch was suddenly distracted by his rotating screen saver images—his two sons, his wife, his dream golf vacation spot in Scotland, his favorite movie still from *Citizen Kane.*

"I said, agreed?"

"Yes, agreed!" shot back Mitch.

"Alright, now we can get down to business! Here's the tip of the iceberg." Graham paused. "Look, I know I've sounded like a broken record for the last nine months or so, but I just had another informal chat with Maxy. Mitch, you're gonna have to step it up if you want to keep this one around. That's all there is to it."

Mitch didn't know that one single second could hold so much silence, but he recovered. "Ah, my multi-faceted friend. Just when you're on a roll, you go and get serious on me!" Mitch said with feigned and completely transparent lightness.

"You can count on me!" Graham quipped. "1:00? Lunch. Come on. We'll do the chat."

Mitch breathed an audible sigh and simultaneously wondered how Graham could use phrases like *do the chat* and still maintain professional credibility. "1:00. The Deli."

"Meet you in the hall. Now, quit tapping that damned pen and get back to work," said Graham, right on the mark.

"Listen, Graham, I've got something else on my mind, too. I actually need to run something by you."

"Of course you do, Boss Man," Graham said. "I'll be all ears."

Mitch tapped the keyboard, and his screen came back to life. He stared blankly at it for a moment and bit his bottom lip. Noticing the time, 12:30, he reasoned that the next half hour would best be spent considering how to manage the tasks at hand.

Swiveling his chair to the window to see the city beyond and below, all he saw instead was Maxine Rockwell, President of Marketing. He recalled her grand entrance into his life over nine months ago. At a stunning 5'8" in low heels, she strode into his office for an interview flashing that dazzling smile. The only part of her introduction he actually managed to hear was, " . . . but you can call me Maxy," as she extended her hand for a firm handshake.

She sat across the desk from him and talked about what she sought in a prospective employer. In response to Mitch's questions, she used phrases like *room for personal growth that will reflect positively in the growth of the company, opportunities to find creative strategies and solutions to the pragmatic challenges presented in the global marketplace* and *taking on the kinds of challenges that will integrate all departments toward a common goal.* She added that she had consistently "outgrown" each of her previous positions and was looking for a place to hang her hat. She felt that this company may be the place to do so.

As she paused to tuck a strand of straight, light brown hair behind her ear, she asked quite matter-of-factly, "So what would you like me to know about you, Mr. James?"

Mitch felt himself falter for a split second, but quickly grabbed some company rhetoric from the top shelf of his brain saying, "Our mission here is to streamline global trading processes for our clients and to help make them more profitable." He concluded with the fact that Global Trade Management Corporation was poised to be the top international trade corporation in the world.

It later occurred to Mitch that, of course, Maxy was well aware of these facts and that was why she was there. At the time, though, he was puzzled by the look on her face that indicated she was looking for more a substantive answer to her question. Now, sitting there in his office, he realized that the look she'd given him had made him feel exactly the same way he felt when Graham spewed out those little comments that left him hanging, feeling like he was supposed to draw some sort of conclusion from them.

As Mitch shook off that thought, he figured he'd saved the interview when he concluded with telling her, "I run a very tight ship and don't get bogged down in minutiae. I have a very clear vision of where this company is going and I'll do whatever it takes to get us there." He thought the way she'd nodded and narrowed her eyes slightly meant she saw the potential. He also recalled how whole-heartedly Bob, the Chairman of the Board, had supported hiring Maxy. With a big, paternal hand on Mitch's shoulder, he'd told him that while he realized that together they faced the challenge of retaining key talent, she was "just the sort of A-player that this company needs to bring us—one of the biggest and best comprehensive trade controls management consulting companies in the world—to greater success in the broad scope of disciplines in which we operate." Bob felt that Maxy would provide the impetus to formulate a talent retention system, that together the Board and Mitch would use this step as a firm platform on which to build.

Mitch agreed enthusiastically and shortly thereafter, had the pleasure of giving Maxy the fated phone call. As he hung up the phone, he suddenly felt the momentum that this woman would bring with her to the company; everyone was aware of it.

The next week when she left the boardroom after the introductory team meeting, Stephen, the Corporate Financial Officer, said coolly and offhandedly while cracking the knuckles of his well-manicured hands, "Sex in a Suit. Hope we can keep her around." In that very moment—in his general repulsion for Stephen—Mitch realized that it wasn't a blatant sexual attraction that he felt for Maxy. What did, though, come blatantly rushing back to him, was the memory of his college girlfriend, Rory. She'd had that same blinding smile.

With that sobering memory—and a wave of nausea—Mitch looked at the clock, shut down his computer and headed out to meet Graham for lunch.

Unrest

It is not uncommon during a growth phase for a leader to feel a sense of unrest, a subtle, troubled feeling inside saying that something in life is not quite right. **Unrest** creates a disturbance that causes even the most savvy of leaders a great deal of ambiguity, self-doubt and a sense of foreboding that some future misfortune is just around the corner.

Although unrest can feel quite heavy...even annoying at times...a subtle disturbance in the mind and heart is not always a negative. In fact, unrest is often a sign that a positive life change or growth phase is getting ready to take place. A leader's ability to effectively deal with unrest is a critical emotional skill required for success in today's quickly changing world and is directly proportional to a leader's ability to embrace it (not try to squelch it) as a starting point for growth.

During times of unrest, spend 30 minutes journaling, and answer the following coaching questions for reflection:

- Describe in detail the life challenge, business problem or phase of transition that is causing this current feeling of unrest.

- What are all of the "unknowns" that you are experiencing at this time?

- What quiet conversations are you having in the back of your mind?

- When have you felt this feeling of unrest in the past? What happened in your life following this period of unrest?

- Where do you see this period of unrest taking you? (A new level of learning, a more meaningful relationship, better clarity, growth, a life transition, a new career.)

- What steps can you take today to embrace this unrest as a starting point for growth?

TWO | Disclosure

On his way down the hall, Mitch stepped into Leslie's office. As the head of Human Resources, she'd been more of a fixture in Mitch's day-to-day operations over the last six months than he cared to admit. As soon as he came through the door, before he could get a word in, Leslie stood up and headed to meet him, straightening her smart red suit jacket over the top of her skirt. It always seemed to Mitch that she was unnecessarily self-conscious about the extra ten pounds or so that she was carrying since the birth of her daughter. Leslie was 85% business mixed with just enough southern charm to make you feel you could invite her to a family picnic and rest assured that she'd bring the fried chicken.

"Hi, Leslie. No, no need to get up," Mitch said, with her already standing before him. "Hey, before the end of the day, I'd just like to go over the latest exit interview with you. I'd really like to compare your notes with mine, you know, just go over some of the finer details, for the sake of my own records. Routine stuff, you know, before I talk to the Board again."

"Of course, Mitch, I've got the folder on my desk all ready for you," Leslie said, with a completely predictable smile and a perky nod of her blond head. Mitch had started to notice that she regarded him with what he considered an almost maternal concern and he didn't like the inklings of resentment that were brewing in him. The way she tilted her head and nodded—even biting her lip just slightly—

as he talked, told him that she knew this exit-interview rehashing routine all too well. He felt like a boy giving his worried mother a worn-out alibi for his shortcomings or something. Adding insult to injury, he knew his "own records" were not, indeed, his own anymore. The revolving door through which employees were coming and going had become fodder for water-cooler moments of gossip.

Still, Mitch felt some relief in knowing that Leslie prided herself on not being one to partake in interactions she considered juvenile and counterproductive. Her impressive resume of community and civic involvement (beginning at age 7) lent her a more objective perspective of interpersonal dynamics than your average corporate HR director. Luckily for Mitch, the solid double line she drew to protect his image blurred at the intersection of personal and professional. She had a keen eye for potential and a warm, soft heart that melted the edges and barbs of cold, hard facts. Beyond pure altruism, though, was the fact that deep down, Mitch knew she saw the comings and goings of employees as a direct reflection of her own performance and so, she feared, did the Board.

Mitch turned to enter the hallway, and Leslie walked him to the door, pausing in the threshold. "Have a good lunch," she said to his back, lightly touching his elbow as he turned to walk down the hall. He smiled over his shoulder and knew by the distinctive clicking of Italian made shoes that he was about to run into Stephen. Mitch uttered a cordial but obligatory, "Stephen," with a little nod of his head. Stephen responded with the typical hand-to-the-forehead, sans-eye-contact salute that the entire staff—with the exception of any and all attractive females—had come to expect from him.

Mitch wondered on a daily basis what exactly it was about his CFO that he disliked so intensely. He'd known plenty of guys like him, most notably the good-looking, cocky captain of his college soccer team, and he'd always been able to let it all just roll right off of his back. There was something about this guy, though, that shot straight into his solar plexus at every turn. Bottom line, however, Stephen was a damned financial genius. And the bottom line was exactly where Mitch chose to focus.

BEA FIELDS, COREY BLAKE, EVA SILVA TRAVERS

Right on cue came Graham around the corner, dressed, as always, like one of those colorful traveling-billboards-on-a-truck—the kind that are so colorful and vibrant, you can't help but take note of them. Today it was a yellow shirt with a multi-colored tie that looked more like a piece of baroque art. Mitch smiled to himself and wondered if auto insurance companies shouldn't add, "How many traveling billboards are you distracted by on your commute to work each day" to their list of questions when determining a quote. He figured that anyone who lived in a 10-mile radius of the route where Graham walked his dog every day should have outrageously priced premiums due to the visual hazard.

"Hey there!" Graham said, as the two met.

Stephen moved to stand beside Leslie in the doorway. "What, no picnic today, boys?" he called after them as Leslie rolled her eyes. Stephen was referring to the gourmet, homemade leftovers Graham frequently brought from home and shared with Mitch on the patio, weather permitting.

"Not today, Steve. I'll send an IM to your MySpace account in advance of the next one, though, so you can make a notation in your little black book," Graham said with a good natured smile as he and Mitch kept walking.

"Great, great, I'll keep an eye out..." Stephen came back sarcastically.

Stephen hated to be called Steve, and it was far beneath him to join the pop-culture online community or anything else reflecting popular trends. Mitch was acutely aware of both facts and just loved watching Graham make playful attempts at diluting his stubbornly blue blood.

"The Dynamic Duo strikes again!" Mitch barely heard Stephen's jab and looked over his shoulder to see him leaning over just a bit too closely to Leslie. Mitch gave her a look that said, *Sorry to leave you alone with that guy in close proximity!* and saw her give Stephen a light, backhanded slap to his shoulder as she turned and went back into her office with a not-so-subtle closing of the door behind her.

"So, what's goin' on in your world, Mitch?" asked Graham, stirring his passion fruit iced tea.

"Oh, you know. Keeping up with the boys' school and sports. Anna's business is growing like crazy..."

Graham took a bite of his chicken and gorgonzola salad. "Mitch, come on. We're away from the office."

"Yeah. Well, as always—and I know I don't need to say this—but..."

"...this is purely confidential, just between you and me," Graham completed Mitch's sentence. "You know one of these days I'm gonna get downright offended that you still think you have to say that to me. And then where will you be? I'll withhold my gourmet leftovers, and you'll be stuck here at the deli day after day after day. You'll come back to the office smelling like a smorgasbord of warm cheese every afternoon. No one will want anything to do with you. You'll be screwed, my friend."

Mitch laughed and finally moved his glasses up onto his head. "Damn you. You know, I guess we do leave here smelling like cheese, don't we?" Mitch asked, sniffing his sleeve. "We've gotta find another gig! The dry cleaning expenses are killing me!"

"I'm tellin' you!" Graham said.

Mitch took a deep breath. He leaned back in his chair and crossed his arms over his chest as he asked Graham, "So, what do you think of coaching?" He punctuated his question by pressing his lips together.

"Coaching?" Graham repeated slowly. He was seldom caught off guard, but Mitch could see the wheels turning in his head. "Coaching," Graham said, as a statement this time, rather than a question. He sat back, mirroring Mitch's position, but rubbing his chin with one hand. "Well coaching is an interesting phenomenon." He spoke slowly and intentionally, like he was trying to buy himself some time to figure out where Mitch was coming from. "Coaching, I suppose, is leading by example. Inspiring. Drawing out latent talent. I guess you've gotta be tough to coach and maybe both tough and pliant to be coached...in any discipline."

"Well, thank you for the definition, Mr. Webster, but that wasn't exactly what I had in mind."

"Yeah, I know."

"Okay, here's the deal. I'll just...I'll just put it out there and you tell me what you think," Mitch stumbled.

"That's the way we do things around here."

Mitch pushed his sandwich away, resting his elbows on the table for a second, and then crossed his arms again. "This whole talent retention thing. Maxy. Our track record over the last six months. All of it. Well, I was talking with my friend Carl—you've met Carl—and telling him about the scenario."

Mitch continued. He reminded Graham that Carl was the CEO of a much smaller but very successful corporation whose numbers and place in the market had improved dramatically over the last eighteen months. They were attracting talent from larger corporations...and keeping them.

"I had dinner with Carl last week. I wanted to know how he was doing it, you know," Mitch continued. "Well," he paused, "he said that he hired a coach."

He waited for a response from Graham. With his left arm still crossed over his chest, Graham nodded his head, narrowed his eyes, and with the other hand, pulled at his right earlobe in the way he always did when he was carefully considering something. Mitch always found this posture a little annoying. It looked to him like some pseudo-sensitive attempt at palliating him. Frankly, it reminded him of a pose his father assumed before reading him out and punctuating his answer with a sometimes metaphoric but frequently literal, "What the hell are you thinking?"

"And the coaching was beneficial," Graham said.

Is that supposed to be an inquiry or a statement?, Mitch wondered, tapping his fingers on opposite elbows. Whatever it was, it sounded condescending. The thought of replying made him feel defensive, but he answered anyway. "Well, yes. I mean in his case it was."

"So, what are you asking me?" Graham finally said.

"Well, I..." Mitch was getting exasperated. "You're more into this kind of thing than I am. You're the yoga, occasional wheat grass, self-actualization guy. Me, I'm a hands-on, nuts and bolts kind of guy. I work really hard and I work well. I just think the whole idea is ridiculous, to be honest. Watch, I hire a 'coach' and the next thing I know I'm spilling my guts on some afternoon talk show or something. Business is business. I don't need a marriage counselor and I don't need a personal coach."

"Who brought your marriage into the subject here?" Graham never missed a thing.

"Well, no...that wasn't intentional. I was just using that as an example. You know. This whole self-help thing. I know enough about it to know that I don't need to go there."

"Well, it sounds like you already have your answers. I'm a little confused," said Graham.

"No," Mitch paused and took a deep breath, leaning up on the table a bit. "I respect your opinions. You know that. I want to know what you know about coaching and what you think about it. I got Carl's opinion. I want yours."

With a dramatic pause, Graham leaned up on the table, too, to meet Mitch eye to eye. "In a word, I think it's **fabulous**!" he said with his signature flare.

Disclosure

Disclosure is an art form, and when done with finesse in the company of a **trusted confidante**, it can help a leader to gain insight and come to terms with personal and business issues by engaging in open dialogue and feedback. In Chapter 2, we begin to see the importance of this kind of honest communication for a leader, as Mitch broaches the topic of coaching to his closest friend and most trusted sounding board, Graham, the President of Sales. The sage-like but funny and flamboyant Graham complements Mitch's strengths, shoots straight from the hip and provides Mitch with a safe environment to begin to brainstorm around the topic. In a sense, Mitch is able to "try on" a more authentic and honest leadership style with Graham as he explores the personal and professional issues he currently faces. In this case, Mitch is able to explore the topic of coaching a bit further by getting input from Graham.

Coaching Questions:

- Who is your most trusted confidante?

- What qualities make this person someone whom you can truly trust?

- What is something that is keeping you awake at night that you want to disclose to your most trusted confidante?

- How much information are you willing to disclose at this time?

- What are you hoping your confidante will provide you? (Clarity, support, an opportunity to just listen without judgment, advice, a new perspective?)

- What do you want to personally achieve from this disclosure?

THREE | Reality Check

On this particular afternoon, Mitch wasn't quite sure what to expect from Bob. The two men had been working together long enough that Mitch knew Bob's schedule. If Bob had any impromptu requests of him, they usually came his way in the mid-afternoon, generally on a Tuesday or Wednesday, when the scope of that week was gaining focus and momentum. This request, however, had come at 9:30 on a Monday morning.

Feeling rather foggy yet and running a little late, Mitch had answered Bob's call to his cell phone while pulling into the parking lot. He made his way quickly but a bit uneasily to the office. With coffee and briefcase still in hand, he headed straight for the comfort of one of the two matching, big, cushy wingback leather chairs that faced Bob's desk. The scent of the well-worn leather reminded him of the chairs that sat before the fireplace in one of his favorite scenes from *Citizen Kane*. Without being too obvious, he loved to press himself as far back as possible into the cushions, displacing them just enough that their earthy but distinguished scent wafted up all around him. It smelled to Mitch like old money, an association that both invigorated and intimidated him at the same time.

"Mornin', Mitchell," Bob said.

"Top o' the mornin' to you, Sir!" Mitch said, mustering up every bit of energy he could manage. Taking a sip of coffee, which was now lukewarm following the commute from home, he choked and resisted the impulse to spew coffee in the general direction of Bob's cherry wood desktop. *Good God!* he thought, as he turned the Laugh Factory logo on his mug squarely toward himself and lowered the cup inconspicuously to his lap.

"You okay?"

Mitch swallowed and tapped his chest. "Fine, fine, yes."

At home the mug sat without notice between the boys' character mugs, various theme park plastic cups, and Anna's myriad coffee cups with phrases like, "World's Greatest Mom," "Carpe Diem," "Never let the bastards get you down!" and the like.

Bob was seated at his desk. "So, first of all, I want to apologize for calling you right off the bat on a Monday morning."

"No, no need to apologize, Bob, really."

"You know, Mitch," Bob continued without really having heard Mitch's reply. "We really are doing a decent job *overall.* Our numbers are consistently better than most of our competitors. We're attracting new accounts on a regular basis."

Feeling the need for an obligatory response, Mitch said, "Right, absolutely," after which he waited for the *but* part of Bob's address to him. As much as he knew what was coming, he also knew what would follow it, or at least he thought he did.

"What remains a mystery to all of us—and I know that I speak for you here, as well," Bob added, looking to create some empathy, "—is why our key players are dropping like flies."

"I know," Mitch said, looking down and shaking his head. "Mark is just the latest link to drop off the chain." He rubbed his chin and looked up at Bob. "I've got a plan for an incentive program that I'd like to integrate into the Talent Retention Program that I'm formulating. I'd like to discuss it with you before the next Board Meeting." Mitch felt relieved that he had something concrete to offer at this moment.

"Well, sure," Bob said in an unintentionally dismissive tone that sent Mitch further back in his chair. As Bob rounded the desk toward him, Mitch crossed one arm over his chest and rubbed his chin. He'd never seen Bob sit on the edge of his desk before.

"Mitchell, we are poised to be the top international trade company in the world, and you are the star in the center of our universe. We need to make sure you light the way."

Mitch suddenly felt like a child being told on the surface how smart he was when really he was being asked why his grades weren't better.

Bob moved to the other chair. Mitch adjusted himself without even noticing the scent of the leather. He placed his mug out of sight on the floor next to his briefcase.

"Look, Mitch. We're just... We're missing something in the equation here. And I say *we* because we *are* a team. An executive team. You're at the helm, but we're all on board with you."

Mitch had nothing to say, so he just waited. Bob leaned forward, placing his elbows on his knees and touching together the fingertips of his hands. As frustrated as Mitch was right now, something in Bob's posture seemed sincere and supportive to him. Mitch leaned forward a bit.

"What do you know about executive coaching, Mitch?"

Mitch breathed out an audible sigh. His head filled briefly—albeit quickly—with conspiracy theories as he recalled having this same conversation with Graham at the end of last week. He considered but quickly dismissed the urge to ask Bob if he'd been talking to Graham.

"I know that coaching is a popular **trend** right now," Mitch finally concluded. He sincerely believed that smaller corporations like Carl's hired coaches in an effort to try to keep up with the big boys. Global Trade Management was, in Mitch's estimation, one of those big boys that set the standard. He finally gathered himself and concluded, "The last corporation I worked for before coming here hired a couple of different *consultants* at different times to address specific issues. But, the bottom line is that we're already at the top of the heap. Our internal issues can be addressed internally, I feel."

Bob tapped his fingers some more and pursed his lips. To Mitch, his boss appeared to be trying to remember what he'd planned to say next, rather than considering what he'd just told him.

"Look, I've been doing a little research of my own—along with several of the other Board members. Mitch, major corporations are routinely and effectively integrating coaching into their business plans—and with impressive results."

Several of the other Board members?! Mitch thought. The conspiracy theory reared its ugly head again.

"Look, I'm not going to pretend that I know what this whole thing is all about, Mitch. I've attended several seminars where coaching was one of the subjects covered...Marshall Goldsmith, in fact. He was great. I have seen a few of the columns he has written for Fast Company, and I've read some articles on executive coaching. But you and I both know that deep down, I'm an old-school business-man. I'm not looking to reinvent the wheel here. But maybe, just maybe, we can make it turn a little more smoothly and quickly." With that, Bob sat back in the chair and crossed his arms across his broad chest.

Enough said, Mitch gathered by his posture. "What's my next step?" he asked.

"Well, I've got a list of the top three coaches in the area. They've all got impressive resumes. You know it's only the best for my CEO!" Bob said with a light chuckle, trying to lighten the mood a bit. "Gather your wits, you know, interview them. See what you think. Consider this move a potential support mechanism."

"Fair enough. I'll call them. I'll get back to you," Mitch concluded with a quick nod while wondering where Bob had gotten the phrase *support mechanism*. It made him feel like he was being invited to some 12-step program.

"Great. I appreciate your cooperation, Mitch. I really do," Bob said, extending his hand for a shake. "Oh, and I've prescreened them, talked to them about our situation. They'll be expecting your call."

Our "situation"? thought Mitch. *You've talked to them already?* "Well then, I will follow through, as always. Consider me on task."

Reality Check

Frankly, it's quite common for leaders to let power and position inflate their egos... some more than others. It happens frequently with leaders who are the A-players of the world, the superstars who demonstrate the competence and determination to go the distance and get the job done, often by working long hours and performing seeming miracles for the company. All the while, board members reward the leaders' performance with big-money promotions, pats on the back and endless commendations. These leaders have been tenacious and unyielding, using charm and charisma to persuade all stakeholders of the company to move in the direction of an inspiring vision.

Such circumstances present the ideal situation for a virtual halo to develop around the leader. The leader is positioned on a pedestal as someone who can do no wrong, and at every turn, the feedback he or she receives is not merely positive—

it is frequently unrealistic, even borderline surreal. In light of constant praise, a top-performing leader can develop behavioral blind spots. In Mitch's case, "over the top" praise has rendered him numb and clueless to the fact that a few negative behaviors—subtle as they may be—are causing him to lose his edge. The halo effect has created a veil between Mitch and his flaws. It prevents him from seeing that he is descending into a downward spiral and is taking the team and the company with him.

Our protagonist is not alone. This phenomenon happens every day with leaders of every role imaginable, from major corporations to small businesses to non-profits and grassroots organizations. So what do you do in a situation like this? You give the leader a reality check before a major life consequence does it for him. If you are the one **given** the reality check, listen...and listen well.

Coaching Questions:

- When was the last time you received a "reality check" about your leadership skills, your behavior, or your choices in life?

- How did you receive the reality check? Did you hear it from another person, through your own self-awareness, from a book or movie or a major life consequence?

- How did you respond to the reality check? What did you do?

- Now that you can look back on this reality check, what did you learn? How have you grown as a result?

- Where in your current business or personal life are you experiencing struggle?

- What are you doing or not doing that might be contributing to this struggle?

- What next steps can you take in order to perform a reality check about what's really going on for you? (Get feedback from the people in your life? Talk to a trusted friend or advisor?)

FOUR | Rejected

On his way into the office the next morning, Mitch stopped in to the lounge to refill his coffee mug. Not one to consciously repeat mistakes, this morning he'd made sure he had the stainless steel travel mug that Anna had gotten him for his last birthday. Elizabeth, Mitch's COO for the last 18-months, had the same idea of morning coffee. Leading by example, she'd instilled in him—and most of her colleagues—a love of gourmet coffee, and had even gone so far as to gift the office with its own industrial coffee grinder for Christmas. Mitch enjoyed the tutelage that Elizabeth offered on fine imported African-Arabian coffees. In return, when on business trips or at conferences, he offered his insights on which high-end vodkas make the best martinis. Following Elizabeth's lead, the Board had seen to it that their staff had "ready access to all of the caffeine they can handle." That's how Graham had put it, anyway, when the espresso machine was delivered on December 15th that same year with a big red bow on it. Most of the staff members enjoyed their various espresso drinks, but Mitch and Elizabeth loved good old classic coffee.

"Wait, wait...don't tell me," Mitch closed his eyes and waved his hand toward his nose breathing in the heavy aroma as he moved toward the counter. "An imported dark blend this morning, right?"

Elizabeth laughed. "No chain store coffee for this crew. This, Sir, is an Ethiopian blend."

Mitch poured himself a cup—black, no cream and no sugar. Occasionally he'd let himself enjoy a little raw sugar, but he usually liked to take in the rich full flavor in all its splendor. "Ahhhh," he said, taking a sip. "And, wait, the growing regions..." Mitch paused in thought. "Sidamo, Harer, and Kaffa! And you **cannot** tell me otherwise, because once I learn something," he tapped his forehead, "... there it stays!"

"Very good!" Elizabeth said, with a conservative nod of her head, not nearly matching Mitch's enthusiasm.

"Elizabeth," Mitch said, taking a longer sip this time, "what would I do without you?" He was referring to the coffee, but the look on her face told him she took that rhetorical question for every nuance of meaning she could assign to it.

"I shudder to think," she replied, as usual, with a smile.

"You and I need to talk about how to proceed with the Harkins account. They've moved their base of operations from Japan back to the states. We need to be very clear on the details of how we move ahead."

"Great," Elizabeth replied. "I'm available when you need me."

With that, in came Jonathan, smiling widely and rubbing his hands together. "Hey, mornin'! Damn cold DC weather can't stand up to Elizabeth's Special Brew!" With blue eyes, sandy blonde hair and a sort of Abercrombie style, the young President of sales looked more like a hip California guy than an east coast businessman.

On his heels came Stephen. "Mitch, Jon, good morning. And Liz, you're looking as good as the coffee smells."

"Don't call me Liz."

Jon caught Mitch's eye with a look that said, "The guy just never learns."

That's my cue, thought Mitch, as he left the room.

Back in his office, Mitch snickered to himself. *I've got a great staff. Not only are we doing a great job...we keep each other amused, too! I'll meet with Elizabeth later today. I'll fine-tune the Talent Retention Program for presentation at the next team meeting. We're on a roll.*

Mitch figured he'd go ahead and make the calls for coaches routinely as a matter of doing business. Good follow-through. Research was the only thing that he was obligated to do, after all.

He called the first name on the list and felt a little relieved that this initial leg of the research was put on hold by the voicemail message of an all too-perky woman who, he reasoned, was probably younger than him. He envisioned her as fresh out of college with a Masters degree in counseling or something. As far as Mitch was concerned, she had absolutely no credibility. The voice attached to the second name on the list sounded, he thought, like a mild-mannered businessman who seemed a little too sure that coaching was the right step for Mitch. They talked for twenty minutes or so. He seemed like a nice enough guy, but Mitch was not all that impressed.

Signifying the halfway point on his list, was his third contact. By now, Mitch was feeling somewhat smug and rested a little easier in his chair, leaning back a bit and tapping his pen over a crossed leg absentmindedly. He pictured himself at lunch with Graham, rattling off the list of names he'd gone through and how none of them had a damned thing to offer the CEO of an internationally recognized—if not revered—company like this one!

"Good morning. This is Kate Nelson." The voice was warm but professional. It caught Mitch off guard a bit, and he sat up a little straighter.

"So, they've told you about me," he added after their initial greeting.

Kate explained that no, she'd actually not gotten much information about him and that when Bob called, he was really inquiring about Kate herself, coaching in general, and what she had to offer.

Mitch wasn't sure whether to feel relieved or disappointed. He picked up the pace with his tapping pen and tried to collect his thoughts. "Well, very good, uh, excellent. I'm interested in hearing a little bit more about what you do and how you can—well. I just want to know what you do and how..." Mitch paused and took a deep breath. "Honestly," he said, and it sounded more like a question than a platform to continue with his feelings. "...I'm a bit skeptical and I'm just gonna be candid with you about that. I run a very tight ship. I'm fairly driven. I feel, uh, I've always been extremely motivated. So, I'm just skeptical about what this whole coaching... leadership coaching thing is, because I really feel like I'm an excellent leader. So, I'd like to hear some more about that from you if we could just go from there."

"Sure, that's great. Mitch, I'd like to ask what is it that you really feel most skeptical about, and I'll address that before we go into more detail."

Mitch was hoping for something more akin to reading-from-a-manual responses than he was getting here. The other guy he spoke to had been very straightforward vanilla about his inquiries. Mitch had to admit to himself, he kind of liked it that way.

"Well, uh, that, that's a great question. I just... You know... Allow me to— permission to be direct, if that's okay." He tossed the pen onto his desk.

"Yes, please. I'm very direct," Kate responded.

"Well, I know just a very little bit about you. I'm not sure of what your back-ground is. I have an **extensive** background in commerce, in international trade. Global Trade Management Corp. is a very high-powered company." Mitch sat up straight to his desk. "I...have you...ever been a CEO? Have you *ever* worked in global trade?" He spoke more slowly now. "I'm skeptical as to how *you* can help *me* or our company reach goals if you don't have the background that I have. That's probably one of the main reasons why I'm skeptical."

Kate explained that, no, she indeed did not share his background, but had a degree in business. She went on to say that she had 18 years in health care consulting, to which Mitch said with a chuckle, "God bless you on that!" and, though Kate laughed, he then second guessed his perhaps ill-timed humor. She added that with her variety of leadership roles in small business and in the non-profit sector, she had decided eight years ago that her cumulative experience would be well-suited for executive coaching. At that point she went back to school. Mitch was impressed with the name "Georgetown University," and its leadership coaching program. Since then, she'd worked with close to 600 leaders and their teams. "I bring a broad skill set to the table to support leaders in finding answers to a variety of leadership questions and concerns," she concluded. Mitch had to agree.

"Now then, some people do prefer to work with a coach who is in their industry. As a matter of fact, I would *encourage* you to talk to a coach or two who is steeped in international business. You may find it helpful to work with someone who is a benchmark for you." It impressed Mitch that Kate was offering unsolicited options. "That might be perfect for you, especially if you want a consultant or a mentor."

"I'm a little confused here. I thought that's what we were talking about. What's the difference between consulting or mentoring and coaching?" he asked.

"Have you worked with a consultant before?"

Mitch explained that much earlier in his career, his company had brought in a consultant and ended up with disastrous results. "We ended up worse than when we started! So, I'm sure you'll understand my hesitation."

"Absolutely. Mitch, let me take a step away for a minute. When your Chairman called me—and correct me if I'm wrong—he described you as the best in the world at what you do." Those were not words that he was expecting from Kate, but he was willing to go with the general idea and give it some momentum.

"Well, I strive for excellence. I am driven and I'm motivated. It flatters me to no end that he recognizes that, because I really am committed to this company."

Kate went on to explain where she was going, adding that from what she gathered in speaking with Bob, consulting was not what he was looking for in the relationship that she might have with his CEO. "Let me clarify. As you just explained, consultants are retained for the purpose of bringing a very specialized expertise to the table. They go into your company, diagnose a problem, and fix the problem, all along teaching you how to do those very things, as well."

"Okay," Mitch said hesitantly, thinking that what he needed was someone's specialized expertise in talent retention.

"Mentoring is somewhat a form of coaching. In your case, for instance, you would hire another CEO with an expertise in international trade. That person would mentor you in the day in/day out skills required to bring greater success to your company. You would invent in yourself the skills you lack or would like to improve based on what your mentor has accomplished."

In the very moment that Mitch winced at the word "lack," Kate met him with what Mitch thought might just be an affirmation. "What I'm wondering is why you would need to emulate anyone else's skills when your Chairman is saying that others seek out your skills."

"Well, thank you. Yes, when I decided to take the position here, I turned down two other very attractive offers and I've turned down several offers since. But I love and am committed to this company. So, having said that, I feel a bit like we're talking in circles. Quite frankly, considering the skills that I bring to my career day in and day out—and it's plain that my assets are recognized and appreciated—I don't really understand what the problem is." Mitch stood and began to pace. "You've used the word *problem* several times. And I don't understand what the *problem* is. I defer to your expertise here, but it sounds to me like coaching is for problematic people, and I'm not..." Mitch paused for an audible sigh and ran his hand through his hair. "Well, I'm...I'm a little put off. Granted, this is my decision, I'm exploring, and I'm interviewing other coaches, but the bottom line is that part of my skepticism about this whole idea is that I don't know what it is that I'm supposed to fix."

"Okay, got it. Well, now that we've covered the differences between consulting and mentoring, let me explain a little about what coaching is, specifically. Coaching is a collaborative partnership that is designed to support you and your organization to take very deliberate actions toward what you want to achieve in your company and for your team...and for *yourself* personally. I am a leadership coach, so with my expertise, I can brainstorm with you so that you are able to quickly troubleshoot areas in the leadership domain, which can be both improved and enhanced so that you and your company get the results you want. Because I have heard that you are the best of the best in the field of global trade, I am going to be holding you as one of the most competent professionals in your industry because that's already what I'm hearing you are. Piggybacking on that idea is the type of coaching that I personally do. I work with leaders who are already very, very successful...I don't specialize in working with problematic people. Some coaches do, and this is not my expertise. I mentioned the word "problem" as it relates to consultants diagnosing a problem in your company. I specialize in working with top performers, with men and women who are moving from success to significance. And...quite frequently, Mitch, the top performers I work with do come to me to brainstorm around what they view as a "problem" or a "challenge" in their leadership or with their team. You are a top performer in your industry...and, because I work with leaders every day, I would just guess that you are not living 'problem free' in your business. That's why your Chairman called me. Is that correct?"

He continued to pace. "Yes. Well, I guess you're right. I have challenges, as does my team."

She went on to explain that from an outsider's point of view, the changes—enhancements, improvements—in Mitch and the ways that he conducts business and leads his team would be very subtle but would carry profound effects. "I might add something else here, too, about problematic people."

"Yes, yes..."

"Well, I've noticed over the years that people who are very problematic do not respond as well or achieve as much growth as people who are high performers like you. So while some folks are not designed for coaching, I have found that top performers love the coaching format, because they know they can grow even more with the support of a coach.   Let me give you an example. Do you know who Tiger Woods is?"

"Of course," Mitch answered, pausing now and halfway sitting on his desk, already pondering the equation at hand.

"Well, Tiger Woods works with a coach that he could beat any day on the course. So, what do you think he is doing with that coach?"

"Hmmm... well...skill improvement, focus, his mental game...and when you swing a golf club, you don't have an external view. That's why they have those computer programs that analyze a golf swing or the gait of a runner, etc., etc. I'm gonna get one of those, by the way, for my golf game! But another time for that..." Mitch said with a sincere laugh.

"Ah, we'll talk about that, too!"

"So, obviously it's for that objectivity. That outside point of view. But isn't that what my Board's for? I have always implemented every single change they've asked for...with excellence. So, I'm curious to hear what more you can offer than that, how your perspective will be different," Mitch continued.

"Yes...your Board does indeed provide you with a very valuable outside perspective, but as you know, your Board has a very vested interest here, so it is not uncommon for some objectivity to be lost when you are as close to the business as your Board is. What I will bring is a truly outside, truly objective perspective. I don't work for your company. I'm not on your Board of Directors." Kate continued speaking more slowly now, "My interest will be you and what you are able to bring to the table. I have been trained with some great skills that allow me to listen to you, to observe you, to brainstorm with you, and to see multiple perspectives to your challenges and goals. On top of that layer, early on in the process, I will also be gathering some information from the people who know you best. I will be asking your permission to speak with your team to get their feedback, too, on this situation because their perceptions of you as a leader will be important to the work that you and I do together."

Just then Graham popped his head in the door. Mitch covered the phone and said softly, "Well, speak of the devil!"

"Moi?!" Graham mocked.

Mitch hadn't even noticed the time. He pointed to the phone and shrugged; they'd have to do lunch tomorrow. This call was taking longer than he'd expected.

"Denied!" Graham huffed out with the usual, intentional theatrics. Mitch was at once grateful for the momentary distraction and curious about what else Kate had to say, much to his own surprise.

"...and finally, everything that you and I discuss will be strictly confidential. If you and I decide to work together, I will not even be able to tell Bob what we discuss. First and foremost, I want to create a comfortable, confidential environment for you to be able to talk as candidly and as openly as possible so that we're able to work on key leadership skills that will be important to both your professional life and your personal life."

Mitch rounded the desk to find his seat again while gathering his thoughts. "You know, you've used the words *personal* and *personally* several times, and I've gotta say... Look, I had a wonderful childhood and loving supportive parents who set me up entirely for success. I have no unresolved issues," he continued, making quotation marks in the air with his fingers. "The idea of addressing personal issues makes this whole thing sound suspiciously like therapy...and I **don't** need therapy. If that's where we're headed, I do not want to go down that rosy path." He was waiting for an answer but thinking, *Yep, I knew it all along! Top dollar, glorified therapy!* "Look, I'm just being frank."

"No, no, this is great. I feel like we're already being very honest," Kate said, feeling a bit invigorated by Mitch's tough questions; Mitch could hear the smile in her voice. "Look, my coaching style is to work with key leadership behaviors that are going to impact your bottom line in your organization. Again, the word around town is that you are one of the brightest and the best. So as we proceed, you and I will discuss the specific leadership skills that you need to be the best that you can be. By leadership skills I mean your communication skills, your emotional intelligence, your ability to persuade, your ability to refine and hone and maintain key talent..."

Without knowing it, Kate struck a chord with the key talent issue. Mitch leaned his head back over the top of his chair and stretched a bit.

"...I'm talking about these kinds of personal and interpersonal skills, not about things like collaborating with you on writing and refining a strategic plan or other such things that you already do well..."

Mitch nodded to himself and thought about Maxy. Kate continued and explained the difference between coaching and therapy, in case there were any lingering blurred lines for Mitch. "Mitch, I also want to state upfront that I do not diagnose therapeutic issues, and I do know when I'm about to step out of the world of coaching and into the role of therapist and I do not cross that line. In fact, in the best interest of the client, I have let several of them go when I've felt that their needs would best be met in therapy and not in coaching. I have also referred my clients out to therapists when I notice a psychological need surfacing that I am not skilled or licensed to address. More often than not, therapy is grounded in some sort of unresolved issue from the past."

Mitch blinked and shifted uncomfortably in his chair. He didn't like the fact that the thought of needing to retain Maxy always took him back in time to Rory and his college days.

"...while coaching, on the other hand, is really designed to support you in moving forward, in taking action, developing credibility and finally in seeing your actions from different perspectives. So, the distinction is that while coaching involves taking a look at the emotional components of your leadership behaviors, we're not going to focus on healing your past. We will be more focused on taking action in the present to get you where you want to go tomorrow."

"That's very, very clear. Thank you. It's also clear to me that you are not the embodiment of what I pictured a coach to be. You're not the clappy-happy cheerleader type," Mitch said with audible relief. They both got a good laugh out of that one.

"No, but there are coaches like that. I have a very straightforward, somewhat direct style, and I customize my leadership coaching for each client I serve. You and I will co-design the coaching at every step of the way to meet the changing needs of your situation, your organization, your team and your goals. I won't come to you with a boxed system, but I will come to you with a very direct, very practical approach. I will not be telling you what you want to hear...I will be shooting straight from the hip so that we can move forward as quickly as possible. What I've found—and I know I'm repeating myself—is that high performers move even further ahead with attention to individual needs and a very laser-like, direct coaching approach. Keep that in mind if you consider partnering with me as your coach."

"Right. Fair enough," Mitch responded. He wasn't used to people being this direct with him, not even Bob. He wasn't sure if he liked it, but it definitely intrigued him.

"I need to clarify one thing along the lines of the *personal* that you mentioned. Mitch, with leaders, I really want to make sure that their personal and professional lives are lining up. I want to make sure that what you are personally aspiring to is matching up with what your organization wants to do. If there is any disconnect in those two, there is a good chance that there will be friction between the two. If I talk to you for hours about just what's going on at work, I'm missing a big part of the picture because..."

"With all due respect, Kate," Mitch interrupted, "how does my relationship with my wife or vacations that we **don't** take together or something along those lines have anything to do with my company becoming the top international trade corporation in the world? And that is my goal."

"Alright. Let me see if I can clear this up. Mitch, do I have your permission to coach you for a few minutes?"

"Umm...well, sure. We're on a roll, I guess," he replied.

"Mitch, something is telling me that you are not thrilled about having this conversation today. So, let me ask you this. What would you love to be doing right now, rather than talking to me?"

Mitch spun his chair away from the window and back to face his desk. "Well, what I need to be doing right now is dealing with some personnel issues at a very high level. We had some turnover, and I need to put some attention to that matter. So, that's what I *should* be doing."

"You just told me you *need* to be doing and what you *should* be doing. What I asked was what you would *love* to be doing..."

"Uh..." *this one's sharp*, Mitch thought. "Okay, I'll play along. Hmmm, well, I'd love to be on a golf course. On a golf course in Scotland. I recently took a trip to Scotland, and we played all of the courses we could find over a ten day period, and it was *fantastic*!" Mitch began to talk quicker and with more intonation. "Do you know that in Scotland, you can take a cocktail out onto the course with you!?"

Mitch shared that outside of that trip, he'd really only played a handful of times in the last year. He had responsibilities, after all, a business to run and a family to provide for, he explained.

"That is an area that I would want to work with you on, Mitch. Getting to see that down time and fun time are actually productive times...that your personal life can support you in being fully engaged at work and add energy to your life as a leader...for you and your company. It sounds like playing golf just once a week could be that kind of time for you."

"That would be terrific. I try to keep those thoughts as suppressed as I possibly can. I don't have time to think about all of the things that I can't do. I have responsibilities," he repeated. "You don't get to the level I've gotten by spending six days a week on the golf course."

"Mmm," Kate responded.

"I'm a little curious as to how me spending an extra day a week at the golf course is gonna bring my profits up," he added with a laugh, "but I'll think on that."

"This is not a question that I think we are going to answer today," Kate said and Mitch bristled a bit. He thought he heard the hint of a smile in her voice and he didn't know what it meant. "Mitch...I am getting the feeling that you are resisting this conversation, and I want to be very candid with you. May I?" she asked.

"Okay."

"As I sit here today talking with you, my observation is that I don't think that you are ready for coaching."

"And, why..." Mitch started to mumble. This was a turnabout that he'd never even considered. This direct approach had morphed into an edge that rubbed him the wrong way.

"I don't think that you're ready to make the decision. You seem hesitant and cautious, which I certainly understand. I know that you have a lot of questions, yet—I sense that you're feeling as if this has been thrust upon you. I could be wrong. What do you have to say about that?" Kate concluded.

"Well, I can say this. Suggestions carry a lot weight when they come from someone in power over you. So, in that sense, yes, I guess you're right, if I have to be *completely* honest. And, banking on the confidentiality of this conversation, I'll say that I do actually feel a bit resentful, a bit like this has been thrust on me by my board. Yeah, sure."

"Okay."

"That's an impressive observation, actually," Mitch conceded.

"Well, I talk to a lot of people about coaching everyday. And from where I sit right now, I would not take you on as a client. I would love, love, love to work with you—you seem like an ideal client for me—except for the fact that you haven't bought into the coaching concept...at least not today."

Mitch was reeling a bit. He expected to be the one doing objective research with the option for denial.

"We may begin the process and end up with you deciding you can't give it your all, which is fine, but I would not be serving you as a potential client if I did not recognize that fact here and now," Kate added gently.

"Well, let me clarify something here and now," Mitch jumped in to his own defense. "If I decide to do this, I will give it my all because that's the way I do everything in my life. I will use every bit of it that I can for as long as it is productive. I will sever the relationship if it's not productive. But I will—make no mistake—I will give it my all if I decide to do it. It just comes down to me making the decision."

"Alright. I have a request. A little something I'd like you to do this week." Kate made her move. "I want you to carve out two to three hours to play golf, even if it's just nine holes."

"Um, okay. Is that a bribe?" Mitch said with a hearty laugh that Kate enjoyed and hoped to hear more of.

"No, no. That's just your fieldwork. What I want is for you to just simply play golf. Then as you're driving back to the office, just start seeing how the golf may give you insight into partnering with a coach. And no, it doesn't take six days a week to get the benefits—as you alluded to earlier..."

"Point well taken..." Mitch said.

"So, just simply reflect on that. On why I would want you to take that time to play golf to help you get the results that you want in your career. I would like for you to e-mail me to simply let me know that you did play golf. You don't need to tell me anything more...just simply...Hey Kate...I played golf yesterday."

"Alright. I accept your challenge, Kate Nelson!"

"Great! And I will be sending you the names of two to three more coaches, because I want you to have all of the options that are right for you. I'll be available by phone or email, if you like, too."

"Well, thank you. I appreciate that."

"I appreciate your time, Mitch. You've asked me some good questions. Have a great day, Mitch.

"You as well."

Rejected

Every human being, at some point or another, has experienced rejection...you didn't get the job, win the contest or attract the girl or guy of your dreams. Leaders are especially seasoned when it comes to experiencing rejection. They are routinely judged on what they do or say, which leads to being either accepted or rejected by their followers.

When considering rejection, look closely at the positive side:

First, rejection, if viewed in a positive light, can actually provide an opportunity for learning and growth and can bring you much closer to success as a leader. When you change your perspective, you can see it as a springboard to gathering information and applying new knowledge that will help you improve.

Second, the majority of our rejections come as a result of our own behaviors, attitudes and actions. The things we do or don't do are almost always responsible for the results we get. It's easy to blame people, the weather or unfortunate circumstances on why we didn't get the job, close the sale or win the blue ribbon. It's much harder to take an honest look at yourself and ask, "What do I need to do, change or improve in order to learn from this experience so that I increase my chances of success the next time?"

Third, if you are a coach, trainer, employer, parent or leader in any other role, don't mislead your followers in regard to how you perceive their skills, abilities and attitudes. Be honest. If you have a client, student, employee, child, etc. who is experiencing rejection from you or someone else, sit down with them and lovingly tell them what you see...not just their shortcomings, but also their strengths. Give them the tough feedback that you know they need to hear in order to **improve**. Most people don't give feedback because they don't want to be hurtful. In actuality, you hurt people by **not** giving them feedback that can pull them closer in the direction of success.

Coaching Questions:

- When was the last time you were rejected?

- What emotions did you experience as a by-product of the rejection?

- What excuses did you make about why you were rejected?

- What behaviors, attitudes or gaps in your skill set contributed to the rejection?

- What changes did you make in your skills or behaviors that created growth, improvement or a positive change in your life?

- Looking back on the rejection, what did you learn?

FIVE | Alone

"Mitch?" the intercom buzzed and Elizabeth's voice came through. Mitch fought to see clear through the clutter that filled his head at the moment, but couldn't help feeling a little annoyed. He felt both surprised and disappointed with himself for nearly snapping back at Elizabeth. He knew she'd be following up on his mention that morning of the Harkins account.

He took a deep breath. "Yes. Hi, Elizabeth. Thanks for being so prompt, as always. I've had some unexpected things land on my desk. Some things that I've just got to wade through this afternoon. Can we discuss the Harkins deal first thing in the morn?" He knew he had an edge in his voice and scrambled for some tag line to divert her attention from it; creating diversions took hardly any effort for Mitch. "Hey, we'll discuss it over coffee! Got any more of that fabulous Ethiopian blend in the cache? You know one of these days, you've got to spill the beans—uh, so to speak—on your supplier. Don't be holdin' out on me now..."

His charm got a consensual laugh, as always. "Alright, Mitch. First thing in the morning. I'll have the coffee. You have the files."

"It's a plan," Mitch answered, and switched off the intercom.

Following his phone call with Kate, food itself had actually been the furthest thing from Mitch's mind, but knowing that his grumbling stomach would be a constant distraction, he'd tried to slip quietly out of the office to grab a quick bite. He'd figured the timing was perfect; Graham would be back from lunch and meeting with his staff by then. So he thought.

"Lunch awaits!"

Mitch stopped dead in his tracks and spun around wide-eyed to meet Graham's smiling face. He'd just left the restroom down the hall from Mitch's office. In that split second, Mitch caught himself and changed his expression to one of confusion and mock disappointment.

"What—I thought you went to the Deli earlier?" Mitch asked.

"What? And deprive you of my Chicken and Whole Grain Spelt with a Thai Butter Sauce? Are you kidding? Sam and I had wonderful leftovers from dinner last night, and you know that I can always put my appetite on hold to share lunch with you!"

"Ugh! Jeez, I—I wish I could, Graham. I've, uh, I've gotta run an errand for Anna today. She can't break away from the office, so I told her I'd take care of some things for her before I go home tonight. Thank you...I'm sorry...I just..."

"Say no more, my friend," Graham said with that nod of his head that spoke volumes to Mitch. He'd seen it before when Graham intuitively knew it was time to put aside the jokes. The nod seemed to mean it was mutually understood that Graham knew there was more at work than Mitch could or would address at the moment, which was both a relief and a burden to Mitch. That is, sooner or later, he knew he'd have to come clean with whatever it was that was making him evasive. That agreement was an unspoken code of their enduring friendship.

For now, though, Graham just chucked him lightly on the shoulder, and Mitch said, "Thanks, man." Once in a while, that expression slipped out of his mouth before he could stop it and made him feel like he was a college kid again.

In the distance, Mitch saw Stephen cross the adjacent hall and witness the momentary exchange with a roll of his eyes. He couldn't help but recall another such instance when Stephen had actually said to the two of them, "Oh, please... save it for the steam room, boys, not the Boardroom!"

*Perfect...*Mitch thought, *my credibility is slammed at every turn.*

With stomach roaring, Mitch went straight to his car, not sure of where he wanted to spend his supposed lunch break in this cloudy and cold weather. Shutting down the CD player before the music had a chance to register, he turned on the seat warmer and rested on the comfortable leather of his Lexus. With his hands on the steering wheel, and the engine running almost silently, all he could hear were the bits and pieces of his conversation with Kate. *Your personal and professional lives lining up..., your ability to refine and hone and maintain key talent..., I don't think you're ready for coaching....*

"What the hell does that mean?!" Mitch said aloud. *It's all a contradiction in terms. They hook you in and then keep you confused so you keep coming back for more. Very clever.*

Feeling a little smug in that conclusion, Mitch backed out and headed out of the parking lot. *I've proven time and again that I'm ready for anything that comes my way. I know how to buckle down and take care of business. I had every option to choose a very different path, but—oh, no, not me. I chose the responsible path. Yeah, she was a little vague about her background. Leadership Coaching at Georgetown University. Okay, I'll give you that. But no business...life...whatever coach is gonna tell me that I'm not ready for...or capable of... anything that I face.*

And so it went in Mitch's head. Before he knew it, he'd driven around the five- block vicinity of the office several times, still unable to decide on lunch. He finally got a drive-thru burger and a Sprite, which was completely unlike him, and called it done.

Back at the office, he figured he'd feel better having had some food to keep him going through the afternoon. When he got Elizabeth's call, though, he realized he was just as edgy, if not more so, than he was before he left in search of lunch. After hanging up the phone, he checked his email, and there it was as promised: the message from Kate with information on the other coaches that she suggested to him. *Very good*, he thought. He quickly clicked on the links. The first website was that of a woman who'd spent 20 years as a CEO in international construction and land development. It wasn't quite what he had in mind, but it was in the ballpark. However, considering Anna's thriving home design and architecture business, he decided against even calling this coach. He told himself if there was one thing he didn't need, it was feeling like he was being coached by his wife.

The next website actually intrigued him a bit. It was that of a man fifteen years his senior who had a resume similar to his, thus far. The more he perused the website, the better it looked to him. Now, if he could get on board with this guy, maybe he'd actually see eye-to-eye with his coach while still being able to please the Board. *The best of both worlds*, he reasoned.

He called James Claypool immediately. He was impressed by the fact that his very capable secretary answered the call. Taking only his contact information, she set up an appointment time for Mr. Claypool to interview Mitch by phone and said she would email him an outline and an overview of the coaching schedule to consider. Great. This seemed so simple. An *"overview,"* thought Mitch. It sounded so safe and objective.

And a few minutes later, there it was in his inbox. A nice, neat little package telling him exactly what was expected of him and when. Not that it wouldn't be challenging in some ways. Mitch did take note that he'd be asked to address certain matters of character that affected his short and long-term goals, but the overview said nothing of his *personal* goals, nothing of "aligning his personal and professional lives." *None of this open-ended, subtle-but-profound change,* he thought. He couldn't help but breathe a sigh of relief. *Thank god.* In his mind it was a done deal.

Still, it wouldn't hurt to give that round of golf a try, he figured. After all, Kate had spent a good deal of time on the phone with him, and he'd promised her he'd be in touch. The least he could do is follow-through with the golfing-as-metaphor idea, or whatever it was. He blocked out a few hours in his calendar on Friday morning. When he called her after that, he could thank her for the golf suggestion and for the lead to Mr. Claypool. That would be that.

On the drive home, Mitch was still annoyed that he just couldn't shake the thought of Kate telling him that she wouldn't take him on as a client. He kept telling himself that hiring Claypool would be the best thing he could do. Still, deep down, Mitch knew that he'd never had anyone be as direct with him as Kate had been. That was his role; he was usually the one calling the shots. He'd set himself up for that role when he made the choices he made in college. *Sure, he'd had employees leave for "better opportunities" and "more potential growth," but those decisions had to do with the company*, he told himself.

Kate's comments, however, were purely personal and specific. Her saying that she didn't work for Mitch's company and was not on the Board let Mitch know that anything more she had to say would remain in the realm of *"personal growth,"* he thought with a roll of his eyes. Pulling into his driveway, Mitch actually felt himself wince at the memory of Kate saying that she wouldn't be telling him what he wanted to hear, but rather what would help him to achieve the greatest degree of progress toward his "personal and professional goals." He absolutely hated the fact that that phrase just created a nebulous glob of touchy feely goo in his mind. *Playing in goo is for children*, he told himself, *and even they need to do so within boundaries.*

With that thought came the memory of his father. *Dad was a successful CEO, and I know damn well that talk of personal goals never entered into the picture!* In fact, Mitch couldn't remember ever talking about personal goals with him.

With the emotional roller coaster he'd been riding all day on the down slope again, Mitch sauntered into the house. He wasn't used to feeling so tossed about and decided he had a definite distaste for this sort of nonsense.

"Hi, boys," he said as he came into the family room, which adjoined with the informal dining area. Daniel, 12 and Kyle, 9 were finishing up their homework before dinner. Everyone was amazed that Daniel's hair had gotten steadily lighter with age. He was sturdy and athletic, "like the men on my side of the family," Anna frequently teased. Kyle, on the other hand, was dark haired and lanky. He loved sports, too, but was definitely the more artsy of the brothers. Mitch liked to believe they'd each gotten the best of his qualities.

The housekeeper/nanny, Emilia, had gotten dinner started, and was just getting ready to leave for the day. Anna was in full gear, taking over in the kitchen. "Hi, hon," he said, giving her a kiss at the corner of her mouth as she turned her head to greet him while chopping vegetables. That's one thing of which there was always plenty in the James' household: fresh organic vegetables. Anna made sure of it, and if she couldn't get to the local, specialty market, she gave Emilia extra cash to make the trek.

Anna had redesigned and decorated the house they lived in. When they bought the place eight years ago, it had been what you'd expect of a traditional two story, turn-of-the-century DC house. However, with Mitch's consent—if not complete support—she'd had it gutted and completely redone from the inside out. Anna liked to joke and say that they'd nearly come to blows over some of the decisions. She leaned toward open-space technology design, which was a far cry from the conservative "brick and mortar" theme, as she called it, that she said had infused her husband's very cells growing up in the area. But, they'd managed to reach agreements that resulted in some rather novel design themes that her friends and colleagues admired. Some of those themes had even inspired and shown up in subsequent work projects for her.

After dinner and some video games, the boys romped for a while with Zoetrope, the family's Golden Lab (Zoe for short). Anna thought it was a ridiculous name and couldn't imagine why Mitch had chosen it. She said that it sounded like an intestinal disease. "I'm suffering with a case of zoetrope," she would tease whenever she wasn't feeling well. But Mitch let her have her little joke and rested quietly and happily in his own personal tribute.

As the boys went off to bed, Mitch reminded them to read for 20 minutes before turning out their lights. Anna kissed them tenderly, and Kyle ran off to grab his latest dragon story. Daniel, on the other hand, gave a mild grumble. Mitch tousled his hair and sent him off. Mitch knew that his son was a budding pre-adolescent boy when he said recently that both he and his dad had hair that was "long enough to be hip, but short enough to be respectable." His elder son had a confidence that he wished he'd had at the same age.

Mitch sat on one of the barstools, tapping his pen on the granite counter top.

"Sorry, hon, but I can't seem to name that tune. Your vocabulary has gotten too wide for me," Anna joked with him. Even when she was tired, she always had at least a glimmer of humor. That was one of the things that Mitch had loved about her from the very start. He knew, though, that this particular habit wore on her nerves a bit sometimes.

"I didn't even realize I was doing it. Sorry."

He was at once looking for an opening to talk with her and hoping that she'd just go off to her office to finish up whatever she had hanging over her head from the work day and leave him alone. She turned and headed upstairs, and Mitch figured he had some time to just sit. Zoe nudged his leg and stared up at him with Kyle's stuffed turtle in her mouth. "No, Zoe. No retrieving tonight, girl." She understood, as always, and headed off to lie by the fireplace in the den.

Anna returned in her silky black pajama bottoms and a mismatched spaghetti strap tank. Mitch loved to see her braless, and she knew it. Tonight, though, he mildly resented the distraction.

"So, how are things at work?" she asked, putting on hot water to heat for her chamomile tea.

"Oh, you know...just..." he sighed, "just the same. I mean, we're still on the upswing in many ways. Just the talent issue, mostly." His conversation with Kate was still ringing in his head.

"Right," Anna answered. She knew the drill and waited for Mitch to ask about her day. She finally poured the hot water into her *Never let the bastards get you down!* coffee mug. "I'm just beat. Expanding the design department is taking every ounce of creative energy I've got. It's exhausting....but, god..." A big grin spread across her tired face. "It's so invigorating, at the same time, you know!?"

Her enthusiasm hit Mitch like a sucker punch to the gut. In that split second, he both loved her and hated her for her passion. He wanted to feel the way she did. He also just wanted her to quit talking and let the straps of her top fall off her shoulders and slip away right there in the kitchen.

"Is that my husband giving me *the look*?" Anna asked, dropping her head coyly and raising her right eyebrow in the way she always did.

Mitch didn't realize he was being so transparent. "I, well..." he shifted on his barstool a bit. "Well, I, normally..."

She reached for the honey to stir into her tea.

"Anna, I, uh..." Mitch cracked his left middle finger. "Do you, do you think that I'm a good listener? I mean, do I consider the things that you say, things that other people say?" He got up off of the barstool and paced a few steps, looking for words, but trying to be as nonchalant as possible. "You know, other perspectives. Am I, jeez, I don't know...open? Available?"

Where the hell is this coming from? was clearly what Anna was thinking when she looked at him. When there was even a potentially sexual opening in the conversation, he never changed course. He knew that anomaly wouldn't be lost on her, and it most definitely was not.

"Mitch, what **do** you mean? I don't..."

"It's just...it's just this situation at work. I don't know..."

Mitch thought that his wife suddenly looked very tired. Maybe even exasperated.

"Oh, come on Mr. Brilliant CEO. Whaddaya mean? Aren't you usually the one with all the answers? That's your job, right?"

Mitch looked up at her with utter disappointment and shifted his jaw in the way he did when words just seemed inappropriate.

"Mitch...I don't...you caught me off guard there." Her tone said she was frustrated.

Since when did you have to be on-guard with your husband? he wondered as he looked back at her.

"Are, are you okay?" she asked a little more softly.

"Fine, fine. Of course. I've just...uh... Yeah, I'll be upstairs in a while." He knew he'd blind-sided her with these questions and practically set her up for failure. *What did I expect?!* he asked himself angrily.

They stood there looking at each other for a long few seconds. Part of him hoped for an embrace or a kiss or something, anything. Instead, he turned and headed into the den to mix himself a Belvedere martini and sit by the fire for a while.

The next day, following his morning coffee and meeting with Elizabeth, Mitch headed straight to Graham's office to set up a lunch date. He'd tossed and turned all night after his martini and awoken with an inkling of conscious resolve to clear some of the clutter in his head.

"So, uh, how'd that *errand* go for you yesterday?" Graham asked over his tuna melt sandwich.

"Right. Yeah, well, let's call that a work-in-progress," he replied, casting a disapproving glance at the mayonnaise dripping out of his friend's sandwich.

"You just described life in general, Mitch. And don't look in my direction with that smug expression. I'm allowed a little saturated fat every now and then. Wouldn't do you any harm, either there, Jack Lalane! Live a little!"

Mitch paused for a second and met Graham's knowing look. "Jack Lalane? You're showing your age there, Buddy!"

"My age is a matter of public record...as is everything else about me," he added with a wink. "The rest of the world can't benefit from reading your pages when you're a closed book, my friend."

Mitch sat back from his chicken Caesar and tossed his hands up with a look that said *where do you get this stuff?*

"I am but a vessel..." Graham said holding his hands palms-up with humility that wasn't entirely mock. "How are you progressing with the coaching research?"

"Well, that's exactly what I wanted to talk to you about," Mitch answered, doing his best to be upbeat and stay on course.

"Mmhhmm. And you can skip the confidentiality clause this time..." Graham teased.

"Ah, yes, I think we've established it. I've made quite a few phone calls. In fact, one of the people I spoke with even referred me to a couple of other coaches. You know, people who have experience similar to mine, who are on the same page and at the same level I am. Aaaannnndddd...I think I found myself the perfect coach. Plus, it'll make the Board happy that I'm following through on their suggestion. You know..."

"Right, right, of course, that's the bottom line after all," Graham said without pausing to think. "God, this sandwich is great."

"What?!" asked Mitch.

"What, what?!" asked Graham, obviously baiting his friend. "I mean, you said it'd make the Board happy. Great. What's more important than that, right? End of conversation."

"That's not what I mean!"

Graham finally paused and put down what was left of his sandwich. "What do you mean, Mitchell? Do you have any idea what you mean? What you're really trying to accomplish?"

Now Mitch was a little confused and a bit pissed off. And he hated the paternal tone of being called Mitchell.

"Alright, let me approach this from another angle. Okay, so let's assume that the Board will be happy. What will it take to make **you** happy, Mitch?"

He couldn't help but hear Kate's words echoing behind Graham's question. "Jeez...you sound just like.... Who says I'm not happy?!" he asked Graham rhetorically. Graham said nothing, but just raised an eyebrow. Mitch continued, "Look, I don't keep a journal; I don't do 'morning-pages'; I don't approach my life the way that you do yours."

"Well, there you have it. You just said it," said Graham.

Mitch grew annoyed with himself because he knew he had a quizzical look on his face.

"I don't **approach** my life—as you said. You make it sound as if you operate from outside of yourself. No, I do not **approach** my life. I am actively engaged in it."

All of the little details of his conversation with Kate were bouncing around in Mitch's head in no particular order.

Graham leaned up to rest his forearms on the table and look at Mitch directly. "And it feels wonderful. And sometimes it feels shitty. But that's just it. It always feels like something." With that, he got up to turn his empty plate in at the counter and get a cup of what he considered to be shitty coffee.

Anna popped into Mitch's mind. He heard her saying how exhausting but exhilarating her work felt to her.

Graham came back with his styrofoam cup. "So, what were you gonna say? You started to say that I sound just like somebody."

Mitch shoved aside his salad and went for a cup of shitty coffee, too. He came back to the table with a handful of non-dairy creamer cups and packets of white sugar. "Shitty," he said, indicating the coffee makings.

"Indeed," Graham said.

"You sound just like one of the coaches I spoke with," Mitch said, sounding wry and a little pissed off.

"And said coach, I'm assuming, would NOT be this **perfect coach** that you've decided upon. Correct?"

Mitch cocked his head, saying all that Graham needed to know.

"Interesting choice, Grasshopper."

Alone

Many people believe that leaders are open and quite willing to turn to trusted advisors and colleagues who can provide them with sound advice on everything from falling bottom line numbers to breakdown in team communication to problems on the home front. In the work that I have done with leaders over the last decade, I have observed the opposite to be true. The majority of leaders (while surrounded by sharp people) do not easily turn to others to ask for advice and direction during tough times. While they are usually quite open to diverse opinions during brainstorming and team meetings, when it comes to making crucial decisions about business or personal issues, most leaders make the bulk of their decisions alone. Why? They believe that sharing concerns and seeking counsel from team and board members may somehow compromise their strength as a leader, making them appear weak and incompetent. They know that, once they begin asking for advice and help from others, they stand the risk of being scrutinized by their followers and employers, who may see them as unable to handle the day-in-day-out challenges and pressure of being a leader. As a result, leaders can often become quite isolated and overwhelmed by the weight of making tough choices in solitude.

Coaching Questions:

- What does it mean for a leader to "feel alone?" Describe the isolation a leader often feels.

- What is a decision you are currently trying to make on your own, without help from another person?

- If you share your thoughts around this decision with another person, what are you concerned will happen?

- When you allow yourself to take a step back from all of the what-ifs and should-haves, what does your intuition tell you about this self-disclosure?

- Who do you trust enough to turn to for support (a coach, trusted friend or colleague)? How can this person most help you at this time?

SIX | Epiphany

As he lugged his golf bag out of the trunk, Mitch wrestled with dueling dialogues in his head. *Who the hell do I think I am golfing on a weekday morning?* was quickly countered by something akin to *Hey, just following the Board's suggestion here!* The day before had been relatively productive at the office, only because Mitch had immersed himself in solo tasks. He also had been happy to report to Bob that he had researched coaches and decided on one that he felt fit the company's goals; he would seal the deal this afternoon.

The home front, though, had proved uncomfortable that evening, and Mitch had avoided any further conversation with Anna. She'd seen him retreat before, but had always been able to joke about it and quote her favorite pop psychologist, saying to Mitch that he was being a man and spending time in his *cave*. This time was different, though. While Mitch called this cave "work stuff," he knew it was a façade. The two spent what remained of the evening casting sideways glances at one another, sans eye contact.

Mitch was actually glad to be out in the fresh, if not chilly, morning air. The sun was bright, and he was alone. No one was making demands of his time or attention. Even brief stops at the gym for a little cardio workout with his iPod strapped to his arm never felt like this. Three words popped into Mitch's mind as he set down his bag on the tee box: quiet, solitude, time. Three things he felt he always lacked. With a self-deprecating laugh, though, he quickly disregarded those words, telling himself he wasn't a Buddhist monk or something; he was a CEO and those three words set a tone that was counterproductive for him.

With that mindset, he told himself it was time to get down to business, play his round and get back to the office. And play he did. Knowing he'd be without a caddy this morning, he'd packed a light bag with just a few of his favorite clubs. He moved quickly through the first few holes. *Just like riding a bike*, he thought. He'd made great progress on his game during his vacation to Scotland with his old college buddies, John and Peter. Mitch's longstanding joke was "With names like those, you sound like my disciples." It had really taken hold when he tutored them during some of their toughest business courses. They both lived in New England now, and the threesome seldom saw one another. For just a few moments on the course alone that morning, Mitch missed his friends. For nostalgia's sake, he did his Chaplin impersonation for no one but himself, swinging his golf club like a cane. After a couple of cocktails on the Scottish green, it had been good for a laugh from John and Peter. Then Mitch quickly outmaneuvered his own stroll down memory lane with a shift in focus to the next putting green and off he went.

After the first hour, Mitch began to glance at his watch with increasing frequency. His game slowed, and his shots lost their edge. His mind began to wander to thoughts of checking email and reviewing a contract or two. He thought of his Blackberry in the car. He wondered how he would handle the residual tension at home that evening with Anna and pressed on through the next hole. His mind jumped back to the office and to Graham. After their lunch on Wednesday, he'd avoided him—and any further conversations of the coaching issue—but he knew that being evasive again today was out of the question, as it would be all too obvious.

After all, he told himself as he placed the ball on the tee, *Graham is entitled to his opinion, but the choice of coach is mine, and the choice has been made.*

Whoosh! Mitch snap-hooked the ball before he even realized what had happened. He looked first in the direction that the ball *should* have gone, knowing full well it hadn't gone anywhere near his intended target. The hook happened so quickly, it took several seconds for the ball's actual path to register with him. Mitch couldn't believe what he'd just done and looked around hoping that no one had witnessed what he regarded as a cardinal sin.

He tried to reenact the swing and pictured himself as a Jerry Lewis caricature. In the moment that he craned his neck trying to actually see what mess he'd made for himself, suddenly and without invitation, Kate's discussion of Tiger Woods appeared front and center in Mitch's conscious mind. *"Tiger Woods works with a coach that he could beat any day on the course. So, what do you think he is doing with that coach?"*

The course suddenly seemed very quiet to Mitch. He closed his eyes for a moment and let the sun warm his face. *Well, of course, it's like I said before. The coach gives him some objectivity, some unemotional feedback. All that,* he thought to himself, tiring of this dialogue and just wanting to get in the last few holes. He opened his eyes and again adjusted his posture to try to see what had gone awry in his swing. This time it was Anna's sarcasm that rang in his head. *Oh, come on Mr. Brilliant CEO. Whaddaya mean? Aren't you usually the one with all the answers? That's your job, right?*

Mitch took an involuntary deep breath through his mouth. He ran his hand through his hair with one hand and put his glasses on his head with the other, as if seeking a completely unadulterated point of view. *No, no I don't. I try to see myself objectively, but I never really fully see myself from the outside...so I never have all the answers,* he thought. He looked around at the groups of people playing golf together. He looked far to his left and saw the people taking lessons. He remembered one of his favorite scenes from *Papillon* when Steve McQueen plays the prisoner and is wasting away after years in solitary confinement. He sticks his head out of the small opening in the door for "inspection." Desperate for human feedback and interaction on more than just his actual appearance, with a haggard voice, he asks the prisoner next door, "How do I look? How do I look?" Mitch remembered how that scene had saddened him deeply the first time he saw it. Now he related to that loneliness.

He'd only had one cup of coffee, but Mitch suddenly noticed that feeling in his stomach, right between his ribs, that he felt when he'd had too much caffeine. His breath quickened a bit. He felt an unfamiliar momentum stir in his chest. He didn't know what he wanted to do or where he wanted to go, but he couldn't focus long enough to continue playing golf. Throwing his club in his bag and lowering his glasses down over his eyes again, he swung the bag over his left shoulder and walked quickly back to the car.

He remembered his last conversation with Graham. *Interesting choice, indeed*, he thought to himself as he pulled out of the parking lot and headed for the office.

"Lunch," Mitch said matter-of-factly as he came through Graham's door. If he didn't know Mitch so well and if he wasn't, in fact, so sure of himself, Graham might have thought—judging solely by Mitch's tone—that he was about to get some kind of reprimand.

Graham looked at the clock on his monitor screen. "Kinda' early, don't you think?"

"If you insist, we can call it brunch."

"Hell, you're the boss. Let's get outta here..." Graham said, slipping a black suit coat over his purple shirt.

"Alright, you made small talk on the drive. Now we're sitting in a new café. You came in this morning without a jacket, never mind the tie. And you seem to have misplaced that chip that was on your shoulder last time I saw you," Graham said, looking quizzically at Mitch.

"I left it in the car."

"The chip?" Graham asked, stirring his iced tea with a straw.

"The jacket. The chip fell off at the golf course this morning," Mitch replied nonchalantly, knowing he'd get a response.

"Golf course? On a weekday morning?" Graham suddenly sat up straight and clapped his hands together. "Candid Camera, right? You've set me up, and we're on Candid Camera. Wait, that's old school. Is it that new show? You know, where they..."

"No, this isn't about your 30-seconds of fame...or mine for that matter. This is about me telling you a story," Mitch said, setting it all up.

"Do tell..."

"At the advice of a, uh, shall we say *confidant*, I took some quality time for myself this morning," Mitch explained slowly.

"Hold it right there, Buddy. You never use the words 'quality time' and 'myself' in the same sentence...unless maybe you were to say *I'd rather slit my own throat than spend 'quality time' by 'myself'*. Even more egregious is the fact that you're telling me you have another confidant! I have been set up. Where's the camera?!" Graham said looking around indignantly.

"Alright, alright. I know this is all a little unusual," Mitch responded.

"A little?"

"Would you let me talk, here?"

Graham waved his hand as if to say, *you have the floor*.

"As you know, I had decided on a coach..."

"Had?"

Mitch had to hand it to him. He didn't miss a thing, but still he gave him the shut-up-or-I'll-kill-ya' look.

"...but had agreed in the meantime to the suggestion of that certain *other coach* I'd mentioned to you."

Graham nodded quietly.

"Well, that suggestion was to play golf this morning, to spend two to three hours on the course. While there, I was to consider how golf—one thing that I truly love to do—could possibly be a metaphor for coaching. Well, I honestly had forgotten about the metaphor thing until..."

The server slowed by their table, obviously eager for them to order and move things along.

"Not yet, dear," Graham chimed in.

"...until I snap-hooked the ball. Yes, yes I know it's hard to believe, but I, Mitchell James, actually snap-hooked the ball."

"I don't find that so hard to..."

"This isn't the feedback portion of the conversation," Mitch quipped. He was in high gear and still feeling the mysterious pseudo caffeine effect.

Graham "zipped" his lips with his fingers.

"When I hooked the ball, I remembered bits and pieces of my conversation with Kate—that's the coach—and with Anna and well, I'll spare you all of those gory details, but suffice it to say that I realized I'd never know exactly how or what I did because I can't truly see myself objectively," Mitch finally stopped for a breath and relaxed into his chair a bit.

"Permission to speak," Graham said.

"Permission granted."

"So, this other coach, this Kate person, she's the one you were referring to? The one about whom I must've struck a chord when I asked you if you really knew what you meant or what you wanted or whatever it was that I said?" Graham asked.

"Precisely," Mitch answered, crossing his arms across his chest. He pondered that idea again for a moment. "So, here's the catch. Here's the real dig. After asking me myriad personal and professional questions, she tells me she wouldn't take me on as a client. Says that I'm not ready for coaching. Haven't bought into it or whatever. I keep hearing that in my head. She wouldn't take me on..."

Graham sat back and listened.

"So, I guess maybe it's time to broaden my perspective a bit..." Mitch continued. "She wouldn't take me on...."

"What else?" Graham leaned up onto the table. "I have a feeling there's a bigger picture here that's concerning you."

Mitch took off his glasses and toyed with them. "I guess I'm wondering if I've made my family feel the same way.....if they don't want to take me on anymore, either."

Epiphany

With executive coaching, one of the ultimate goals is to support a leader in his or her own development through the use of a variety of tools, methods and resources.

I have discovered that, by engaging in life experiences and getting in touch with everything in the surrounding environment, the majority of clients can shift from simply learning extrinsically to experiencing intrinsically an epiphany—gaining a sudden insight into the reality or meaning of something initiated by the experience. Epiphanies create emotional responses in people, and when emotions come to the surface during an experience, the learning is much deeper and longer lasting.

Coaching Questions:

- When was the last time you experienced an epiphany?

- What did you experience?

- What in your environment (or life) was the catalyst for the epiphany?

- What did you learn about yourself, other people or life during this time?

- What changes did you make in your life as a by-product of this epiphany?

- How did the epiphany take you to where you are today?

- What new activities are you willing to experience in life in order to grow as a leader?

SEVEN | Provocation

Following the lunch with Graham, Mitch felt himself juggling more questions than answers; it seemed to be a common occurrence of late, that feeling, and it unsettled him. Walking into the office that morning, he felt painfully and awkwardly aware of the way his briefcase strap felt over his shoulder, the way he squinted his right eye slightly more than his left in the bright morning sun and the way that he walked just slightly more on the outside of his left foot than his right—a result, his chiropractor had said, of years on the soccer field. These observations were unintentional and annoying. They flew through his conscious mind in a way that made him feel defenseless against their assault, like some un-medicated schizophrenic juvenile delinquent. Random, unintentional thoughts were not something that Mitchell James was used to entertaining, not for the last thirty years or so, anyway.

Ironically, this unfamiliar awareness of what Mitch thought of as "little things" compelled him to stay busy enough to reduce their distractions. At his desk, Mitch fired up his computer and tapped out a song with his pen but caught himself and cut short the stupid early 80's tune. His In box both overwhelmed and invigorated him. *Lots to do!* He opened again the intake information email from James Claypool, his would-be coach. He took a deep breath and thought about his conversation with Kate and the golf experience just the morning before. Tossing his glasses onto the desk, he got up quickly, pacing a bit.

Since when has it been so goddamned hard for to me to make a decision?! he asked himself. It was a rhetorical question, but laced with just enough disgust to unsettle his stomach. When he realized that he actually knew the answer to that question, it unsettled his stomach even more. He'd felt such angst twice in his life, once at eighteen when he'd decided on a college major and once as a passionate and confused twenty-something when he chose his course, letting Rory leave for film school without him.

This is ridiculous! She rejected me and now I'm considering how to tell her I changed my mind? Do I want to work with her? Mitch asked himself, eager to think about anything but this coaching choice. Still impressed by the lingering momentum he'd felt since being on the course, he told himself that anyone who gave him permission to golf on a weekday morning couldn't be all bad! With that, he sent Kate Nelson a very matter-of-fact email in regard to beginning the coaching process. Checking one thing off his mental to-do list on a busy Friday, Mitch set about the rest of his day, doing anything and everything to distract his attention from himself.

Mitch held the phone to his ear, clearing his throat several times and adjusting himself in his chair, trying to find a posture that felt nonchalant. It was Monday morning, and Mitch felt that the Board would be impressed with his starting a brand new week this way.

After brief hellos and introductory chitchat, through which Mitch continued to adjust himself in the chair, Kate got right down to business.

"Mitch, I have to tell you that I was thrilled to learn that you changed your stance. I'm happy that we will be working together. It's very exciting to begin this process with someone as well-regarded and capable as you are." Going on to reassure him of his complete confidentiality, she added, "I want to remind you that I am not at liberty to talk with other people about the fact that you and I are coaching together and I am not at liberty to divulge anything to your Board about anything we discuss. So, ask what you need to ask, say what you need to say. I have seen, heard, and witnessed just about anything you could imagine—so there's nothing you could possibly say that would surprise me." Kate said.

Mitch liked her un-patronizing tone. "I appreciate your up-front honesty and your confidentiality. It's essential not only in my business, but also for...well, anything, you know..." he said, sure to avoid any actual mention of his personal life. "You should know that I'm very direct, because I don't have time to be any other way," Mitch said quite matter-of-factly. "I have to say that you impressed me. I was *very* impressed by first, the fact that you were willing to relinquish business by referring me to those other coaches. I think that that's incredible integrity or the most brilliant marketing I've ever seen." Mitch meant what he said.

"Ah...good observation. I have to say it's probably a little bit of both," Kate said with a laugh. Now that he was officially her client, Kate didn't waste any time asking him if he'd completed his fieldwork.

"Ah, yes...the infamous golf game that will save my business..." Mitch said, with searing sarcasm. Kate's silence puzzled him. "Well, uh...I actually was thinking about not doing it—I mean you'd given me the other referrals and, you know. But, well, let's just say, that golf is not a bad carrot to dangle before me. So, duty bound, I proceeded!"

Mitch glossed over how much he actually enjoyed going through the first several holes, getting right to the part when he began to feel antsy. "My mind wandered to emails and appointments and...I still don't really know what happened. Now believe me, there are many improvements to be made on my golf game, but I just do **not** hook the ball! Well...I snap-hooked the ball! And it...I mean, I was focusing on my stance and my swing and my grip. So, okay, I try it again. And I hook it again...this time right into the sand trap. So, by now I'm looking around to see who's watching, right? I crane my neck and try to swing—to try to see what I'm doing—and, you know, it's like a Jerry Lewis instructional golf video or something. Ridiculous!

"And wouldn't you know," Mitch paused for a moment. His tone lightened. "Your voice came into my head, and I was reminded of the Tiger Woods conversation we had. I was thinking how great it would be to have someone to watch me, to see what I was doing and help me correct it. And Bingo!" Mitch said with a snap of his fingers. "I had an actual realization that...at that moment, everything you had said in the previous conversation became perfectly clear about having someone who is outside who sees you objectively. And I got that! I got that from talking with you."

Mitch waited for a response, but Kate seemed to be giving him room to proceed. "Your voice came back to me, and I really saw the value in having a coach at that point. Somebody who is impartial. Somebody who is not in the inner-circle of my business."

Mitch finally sat back and relaxed in his chair a bit. Without touching on the uneasy hyper-self awareness that had descended upon him, he went on to explain the increased productivity he experienced during the day and a half following his morning of golf. "I think it was partially being in the outdoors and doing something that I enjoyed. And—honestly—that's something I never would have done without your prompting. I, uh, I treated it as a directive—to honor our agreement. So, I...I will humbly bow and say thank you."

"You are welcome," Kate replied. "I want to acknowledge you for doing the fieldwork. Mitch, gaining that kind of insight is what coaching is really all about."

He pushed his glasses back up on his nose. "Well, clearly, I did gain some insight. But, uh, I will hold you personally responsible if I now start to regularly snap-hook the ball during my game..." Mitch said with a deep laugh.

"Ha! Well, that's a risk I'll take," Kate replied. "Just know that I'm a coach who offers a lot of creative field work. I am not big on giving gobs of homework... you already have enough of that in your work as a CEO. I am big, however, on using the environment and recreation as tools for your own awareness, your growth and development. I like my clients to use what they have access to around them. Most of my clients are very intelligent and tend to stay in their heads."

Mitch liked being grouped in with *intelligence*.

"Drawing them out into their environments gives them hands-on experiences that broaden their perspectives...and gets them out of their heads. You know, sometimes we all need a little external thunk on the noggin! That can give us those little a-ha moments, like you had."

"And the natural environment is wonderful. Just don't send me out into the woods to sit in a circle with a bunch of other men and beat on a drum while we spill our guts all over the place," Mitch said, wryly.

Kate laughed. "Ah, you're ahead of me there. Don't worry, Mitch. That comes later... Kidding, of course. As for the golf...what do you say now? What in the world does the golf have to do with you building yourself as the leader for an international trade company?"

Damn, Mitch thought. *This one's not long distracted by humor.* "Well, I don't know. Like I said, I was more relaxed. More productive." Mitch hated repeating himself.

"Well, we'll revisit the golf game as we work together...it is one of the best sports I know to get at the heart of coaching, and since this is one of your loves, it's just perfect!" Kate said, and Mitch was glad that his rolling eyeballs didn't make even the slightest sound.

She continued. "What I'd like to do now, though, is to address some of the questions that I had emailed you. I know I asked you not to actually answer those prior to this, but just to toss them around a bit. And we may take some tangents off of these questions, but I want to get through some basics here so that I can get some background from you. So, the first question is what are three goals that you would like to achieve in the next six months?"

Mitch knew the answer to that question long before he'd ever even heard of Kate Nelson, "Well, I'd like to increase gross revenue by 15% and I'd like to create a talent retention plan. Really those are the two."

"Anything else?"

"No, those sum it up," Mitch said. He waited in an uneasy silence, thinking that Kate was probably taking notes.

"How about the next year?"

"The same," he replied.

"How about the next three years?"

"Pardon me? Three years? I, uh, I don't know. I haven't thought that far ahead," Mitch said, a little flustered.

"What are you currently doing in the area of strategic planning?" Kate asked.

"Well, we have an annual plan that we adjust quarterly as necessary."

"Okay," she responded. "Mitch let's talk about you and your *personal* goals. What do you want to achieve in the next three months?"

Here we go again on the personal goals. "Well, I, I think I just told you," Mitch said, getting up and walking toward the window. "I want to increase revenue and create a talent retention plan." He paused and then added defensively, "We need to get the revenues up! I mean we really do. If we're going to be the world leader, we need to do those things. And we need to keep good people around."

"Okay. I understand that those are the goals that you want for your company. Are those the goals that you want for *yourself?*" Kate asked, point blank.

"Um...yes," he replied softly. "I mean this is what the Board wants, these are the goals of the company. This is what I want to work on. This company is, is part of my life."

"Hmmmm....you don't sound too enthused."

"No, I, I, trust me. It's fine. This is, it's what I want to work on."

"Okay...I am going to come back to the personal goals in a minute. Let me shift here...Mitch, what is your vision for the company?"

Mitch sighed. "My vision? To be the top international trade company in the world."

"And how will you know when you're there?"

"The bottom line," he replied. "I mean, we know what our numbers are and we'll know when we get there. It's just the bottom line." Mitch got up from his chair to pace a bit, suddenly recalling Graham's mocking him about *the bottom line* in regard to pleasing the Board.

"What about the talent goal? How does that goal fit into the vision?" Kate continued.

"Oh, well, I know our talent can take us wherever we want to go. And I know, I know we need to work on that. Yes, sure."

Kate pressed on. "So tell me a bit about the talent issue. Tell me what is going on."

Mitch forced a deep exhale. "Well, it's, it's...I guess it's classic industry revolving door. We attract great, top talent. They stay for about a year and then they move on."

"Any idea why they're leaving?"

"Better jobs. Bigger pay. The usual. I'm sure you've heard this all before. It's...it's standard," Mitch said, looking at his chair across the room, but continuing to pace.

"Okay. Anything other than jobs, pay, etcetera? Anything at all?"

"Not that anybody's telling me. No. I always do exit interviews because I want to find out why the folks are leaving. And those are almost always the answers. I mean, once in a while, it's a personal or family reason, but it's almost always those standards," Mitch said, thinking of Maxy.

"Okay. You said that your vision is to be the top international trade company in the world. What is the corporation's vision? This includes the Board of Directors' vision," Kate continued.

"It's the same. To be the world leader in global trade," Mitch answered, feeling like the conversation was becoming redundant.

"You said you'll know when you get there based on bottom line results, right? Is that also how the Board and the rest of your company will know that you've arrived...that your bottom line results are stronger than any of your competitors?" Mitch heard an intercom buzz on Kate's end and hoped she'd pick it up. To his chagrin, she stayed focused on the conversation, and Mitch fumbled a bit.

Mitch had never considered anything but the bottom line in relation to success. "Um, I, I believe so. The numbers are gonna tell us. We know clearly what our competitor is doing. We just have to get our numbers up. It's as simple as that."

"What will being the leader in global trade do for your company, Mitch?"

He didn't know where she was going with this one and asked her to repeat the question to give him time to scramble for something intelligible.

Kate rephrased the question. "Once that day arrives...when the world acknowledges Global Trade Management as the international industry leader, what will you have collectively accomplished?"

"Well, the company has a foundation to provide college scholarships to kids who have the desire but not the means to attend college. So, by reaching our goal, we'll be better able to meet the goals of other people, you know... these kids with goals and dreams," Mitch said, feeling a hint of old sadness as he thought of himself as a kid heading off to college. "So, I'm not sure if that's what you're asking, but that's just one of the things that we'll be able to accomplish."

"Sure, sure. I see what you mean." Kate paused. "Mitch, what is your **personal** vision?"

Mitch hastened the few steps back to his desk, and started rearranging Post-It Notes and pens. "Well, I, of course, I share the vision of the company."

"So, your personal vision is for your company to be the world leader in international trade...you see that for yourself personally, as well. For your company to be the world leader in global trade?"

Silence. Mitch walked back around the desk and took a seat. "Hmmm...I, I don't know. I'll have to think about that."

"You seem hesitant. There's something in your voice and tone telling me that this is not your *personal* vision...that you have bought into it, but it's really *the company's* vision," she said, sounding more like she was asking a question.

"Well, Kate, like I said, this company takes up ...a very sizable chunk of my life. I have a vested interest in it, so it makes sense that I *buy into* the vision, as you say." There was a long pause on the line. "I mean you throw *personal* in there as if... Well, I suppose what I need to do is think about that because it is a valid question. And I, I don't really have an answer for you right now."

Kate was undaunted. "I am going to come back to that in a minute...because as I said in our first call, one of my big goals in working with leaders is to make sure that their personal visions and missions are lining up with the companies' visions and missions."

Mitch sighed in the background.

"Now, I could be totally off here...but there's something telling me your company's vision is not really what you dream about. I am going to come back to that as a piece of field work."

"Kate, I don't really have time to dream. Those sound like luxury questions to me. Like things I'll have time to address when I retire with my pension and my share...then maybe this will be of benefit."

"Mmmhmm...okay," Kate continued. "Let's talk about mission. I've been on your website and I'm learning more about what your company's up to, but can you tell me succinctly what the corporate mission is?"

"Sure," Mitch said, glad to be stepping away from touchy-feely ground. "Our mission is to streamline the global trading processes for the enterprises we serve and, of course, to support them in making the profits they want to make."

"What is your personal mission?"

"Jeez, there you go again," Mitch said, halfway under his breath, but without missing a beat.

"You sighed a long sigh. It seems like my questions are annoying you. Are they?" Kate asked sincerely.

"Well, I...no, as I said, I will go back and consider my vision, but...um, I can honestly, clearly say that I don't have a mission."

"Okay...I understand. Mitch...this is going back to the first call when I asked you what you would rather be doing other than talking to me. So, I'm going to ask you that same question again... what would you rather be doing today?" Kate asked patiently but clearly.

"Ahh...umm..." Mitch paused. All of this thinking-of-unrealistic-options stuff was new to him, new and uncomfortable. "In a perfect world, I guess, I would be taking the day off to spend it with my wife, Anna." Hearing old conversations he'd had with her formed a picture in his mind. "We'd be having lunch at a lovely restaurant down by the water. It's called the Paris Commune in New York City. We'd be having wine. It would be...lovely."

Kate was silent, and Mitch sat with that vision for a moment. Then she went in for the kill. "And would the purpose of that lunch be to streamline global trading processes for enterprises that you serve?"

Mitch burst into laughter. "Ahhh, Kate. You need to work for my company. Very good...well done. Clearly no, no that would not be the mission."

She asked him what would, in fact, be the mission of sharing such an intimate time with his wife.

"To see what happens after the wine...." Mitch said, in his finest French accent, and they both got a good laugh. "Remember, you said this was confidential!" he reminded her.

"Yes, yes..."

"Seriously...Anna is very supportive of me. She's certainly a driving force in the family." Mitch paused thoughtfully. "And...and...I love her. And rekindling that romance would be ...wonderful."

"I am hearing that rekindling the romance, honoring Anna...because you love her, you want to strengthen that relationship. Does that sum it up?" Kate asked.

Mitch responded that yes, that would be the mission of the day and related with obvious affection that Anna works very hard, both as a professional and as a mother. "Perhaps I don't acknowledge that as much as I should, but I try to. A lunch like that would be a wonderful treat for her, too...for both of us."

Mitch felt a little vulnerable and tapped his computer to life, sending the dancing screensaver images off to wherever they went. Kate pressed on. "I'm picking up a certain lightness from you. You make me laugh. You seem to be charming, affectionate, witty and quick and fun...and you have a very...how do I say it...you have a very infectious laugh."

"It's my *charrrriiiisma*..." Mitch said with a smile.

"Yes, you're very charismatic. But I see that lightness come out in you when you're talking about golf and Anna and these things that you love. There's something when we're talking about the company that sounds rushed and heavy. Your pace seems to speed up, and your tone sounds very serious."

"Is it any wonder?!" Mitch replied immediately, reiterating the intense amount of responsibility he felt for his position. "I don't know that I would say rushed and heavy, though. I give my **all** for this company. But we are a multi-million dollar company on our way to the top. That's a tall order!"

"Mmmhmm..." Kate responded, giving him room to speak.

"Don't get me wrong. I am thrilled to be taking this ride...but it's a tall order."

"Yes...I get that. Again, as a coach, I simply notice when there's a tone and/or rhythm change when you are speaking. And...there's a difference between when you are speaking about your personal life and your professional life. That tells me that the two are separated somehow or at least the emotions you feel about the two are different. It's like you are pulling me back and forth into two neatly compartmentalized parts of your life, Mitch. Since I'm noticing that, I want to explore it with you. This is going to be your fieldwork. Do you enjoy writing?"

"Well, I suppose. I don't do much of it outside of work, but I enjoyed writing a lot in college."

"Alright, Mitch. I have an idea I would like to toss on the table. Is that okay with you?"

"Um, sure," Mitch said tersely.

"Okay. This is what I'm going to ask of you. Over the next week, I want you to write an uncensored manifesto. And in the manifesto, I want you to allow what you're passionate about to come onto the pages. Discuss what lights your fire, what ticks you off. What's going on in the world that inspires or frustrates you? What is it that you're drawn to? Is it theater or music or passion with a partner? I want it to be uncensored, just train-of-thought, with everything you think and feel about your life. Are you willing to do that?"

"Okay," Mitch said with some hesitancy. "Could you send an email with details?"

"Of course," Kate said, explaining that she would include about twenty questions that were simply to serve as prompts to get him thinking but didn't need to be addressed directly. "I just want to get you thinking about what you're really up to in life. And it may very well be that your personal mission is 'to streamline global trading processes' and your big vision is 'to be the world leader in global trade.' If so, then I have totally missed the mark, and I will be the first to admit that I am sometimes wrong on these inklings. But something in this conversation today is telling me that there's something missing here. I'm just not sure what it is. And this manifesto will help to open up a few things on this topic…However, the work you do on the manifesto is for your eyes only. I don't expect you to share it with me. Most people like to keep these things to themselves."

Mitch sat back in his chair, feeling some relief in knowing that the call was coming to a close.

"The goal is to just allow things to come out that are not at the surface right now. I just have a feeling that writing a manifesto is a step in the right direction," Kate continued.

"I'm certainly willing to take a look at the exercise," Mitch said quickly.

"Mitch, I'm aware of our time and know that you have a meeting coming up soon. How are you feeling about this call today?"

"Well, it's been interesting... I think I'll give my wife a call later. But, uh, I'm open. I don't think that we've solved the world's global trade woes, but it's been an interesting call. Believe it or not, I am intrigued to find out more and I will do this next exercise with the same curiosity I've had so far," Mitch concluded in the same rushed tone and heavy pace that he felt at the beginning of the call.

"Great, so we'll talk again at the same time next Monday. We'll start that call talking not necessarily about the content of your manifesto, but how the exercise went for you," Kate said, laying the groundwork. "And you can always reach me via email or phone at any time. I'm very available."

"Very good. And you had mentioned something about a 360-Degree Feedback. I'm not familiar with that."

"Yes, I'm glad you brought that up, Mitch. With your permission, of course, I'd like to talk with your team over the next few weeks. There will be about 10-12 key leadership behaviors we will be addressing; competencies that the President of your Board, Bob, mentioned to me on the telephone that the company addresses in talent development... He sent me the list of competencies for your company, and I would like to ask your team how they perceive you in reference to those behaviors."

"Perceiving *me*?" Mitch asked, caught off guard.

"Yes, in certain areas of leadership such as effective communication, authentic leadership, building trust, listening. Those areas of leadership. How do you feel about that?"

"Uh...I have no problem with that," he said somewhat guardedly. "I think they would all answer honestly. I think that I do those things well. Ugh...sure...sure... that's fine if that's part of the process. Again, confidentiality is critical here."

"Yes, confidentiality is critical. I will meet with your team prior to the interviews to explain the process and to assure them of the confidentiality and will be coming back to you with a summary report. I won't be saying who said what. But there will be 10-12 areas that each person will rank you from 1-5 and I will average the scores. They may also add narrative comments. Some people have team members who are very open and choose not to stay anonymous, but people usually choose to remain completely anonymous. Also, I don't use 360's to point out weakness or to be punitive. The purpose of the 360 is for developmental purposes only; to leverage the areas that are really working for you and to improve areas which are possibly creating gaps in your development." Kate explained with obvious confidence.

"One question," Mitch said quickly, having been formulating a question in his mind, "If a certain area of ....*weakness*...." Mitch barely squeaked out the word. "...were to come up and it was person-specific, but I didn't know who it was, it would be rather difficult to address it, right? I mean with that person directly?"

Kate explained that the 360 would look at his team's overall feelings and comments and that it wouldn't focus on any one person's specific satisfaction or dissatisfaction with his leadership. If there seemed to be distinct personal issues that were affecting the team's performance, she could approach the Board about conducting a 360 process for the entire leadership team, simply to hone in on a development plan for the team, but they would cross that bridge only when and if necessary. "Not to worry, Mitch. It's a tool whose process will easily unfold as we go along, and I am very careful to make sure that the process goes smoothly and that I am communicating each step of the process to you and your team and that all questions are answered. The 360 Degree Feedback Process usually yields very positive results for my clients" she concluded.

"Very good. Right. I'm getting ahead of myself. And my meeting is here. Is there anything else?" Mitch asked.

"No, we've covered it. Thank you for your time, Mitch. I look forward to speaking with you next week."

With that, Mitch hung up the phone, took a deep breath, closed the lid of the last hour's conversation neatly and tightly, and headed out to fulfill his next duty.

Provocation

In the late 1990s, Thomas Leonard, founder of CoachVille, LLC and Dave Buck, CEO of CoachVille, LLC began to teach leaders and coaches from around the world about what has become known as one of the most controversial yet effective coaching techniques used by today's masterful coaches: "Engages in Provocative Conversation."

While provocation can incite, irritate and even anger a leader, this arousing of emotion can shift a leader from feeling stuck to actually feeling inspired to take action. In Chapter 7, Kate fires question after question at Mitch. She is persistent, and this process of provocation creates frustration for Mitch. This is actually part of Kate's process...to annoy, incite, and stir up emotions, feelings and responses that will point to new insights for Mitch. When a leader is being provoked, there is usually much more to the story than meets the eye (where there's smoke, there's fire!), and this provocation will most often open up an opportunity for learning for the leader.

Coaching Questions:

- Think of the last time you had a conversation that provoked you. What was the subject of the conversation?

- What about this conversation provoked you? Excited you? Angered you? Annoyed you? Disturbed you?

- What did you learn about yourself from being provoked in this conversation? (Your beliefs, values, stand in life, a possible area of improvement, a new opportunity for growth.)

- What is the most provocative question that someone could ask you about your current life as a leader?

- How would you answer this most provocative question?

EIGHT | Fear

Mitch checked his watch. 9:52, it read. He'd been intermittently pacing, sitting at his desk making notes and drinking coffee for over an hour. More accurately, he'd been slurping coffee and wishing for a direct IV drip, having made two extra trips to the kitchen. Mitch usually liked to sip his java. The taste and aroma of Elizabeth's Special Brew—as it had come to be known—was like the scent of the leather chairs in Bob's office to him. This morning, though, it could have been lighter fluid he was drinking, as long as it delivered the confidence-bolstering effect of caffeine.

Wanting to avoid any preliminary chit chat or questions, Mitch waited until exactly 10:00 before heading down the hall, confident that the entire team would be assembled by then and he could walk in and deliver the necessary information. *Nothing more, nothing less. Simple,* he told himself. He tapped his pen on the side of his thigh as he walked briskly toward conference room A.

"Good morning, everyone!" Mitch said, with a mock enthusiasm that made Graham cringe. "Thank you all so much for taking a few minutes to meet this morning. This...this won't take long. Just want to bring you all up to speed on a few **minor** things," he continued, intentionally stressing the word *minor*.

Leslie nodded and was the last one to sit down, following Mitch's cue.

Elizabeth, with her impeccable posture, sat upright with pen in hand to Mitch's left, ready for any and all notes.

"Now, it's no secret that we're dealing with a couple of issues that we need to address. First, while the numbers are still better than those of most of our competitors, they're not good enough to move us on to where we are ultimately headed.... *to be the top international trade management corporation in the world.*" Mitch saw Stephen mouth along with the phrase while bobbing his head and lost his train of thought for a moment. He cursed himself for a split second, knowing that the team had heard those words from him a thousand times. More importantly, he was beginning to realize that every repetition without any progress or plan of action meant less and less credibility for the company and for himself.

Mitch cleared his throat and continued. "Second, of course, is the issue of talent retention." Jonathan caught Mitch's eye with a smile and a nod that let Mitch know his VP of Sales wasn't going anywhere. Leslie turned just in time to meet Jonathan's look, too, and caught a wink from him.

Relieved to have broken the ice, albeit with a dull pick, Mitch surveyed the rest of the team quickly. The look of boredom on Maxy's face threatened to counteract the caffeine effect, so he quickly looked back to the skeleton notes he'd taken earlier.

"I know that these are issues we've addressed in our weekly team meetings before, but I'm approaching them from a new angle now...and, uh, I want to share some information with you." Bob was seated at the far left end of the table. Mitch tried but couldn't read him.

"After some discussion with Bob, I've decided to work with a coach, an executive coach, to address these issues and help us to get on track. To get where we need to be."

The room fell silent. Bob started to speak, and Mitch actually hoped he would take the reigns, if only for moment. When he, instead, gave his CEO a supportive nod, Mitch swallowed hard and felt himself take a step that he knew would have to be followed by another and another. He saw Leslie tilt her head in that maternal way she had.

"You mean, like a mentor, right?" Leslie asked and then looked around at her colleagues, as if hoping they would rally.

Mitch stammered a bit; his conversation with Kate and all of the touchy-feely subjects he'd skirted with her came rushing back. "Well, no, no. Not exactly. But we will be focusing on what I need to do to address those two specific areas."

"Mitch, with all due respect, I don't understand—" Elizabeth said, appearing frustrated. "We are an amazing team. You have all of us at your beck and call. Why do you need to bring in someone from the outside? I think that we all give each other great feedback on just about—"

At the mention of feedback, Mitch recalled his a-ha golf moment and Kate's Tiger Woods example, but he didn't want to get that personal with the group.

"Communication is not our strong point, Liz," Stephen interrupted.

"I'm addressing Mitch, Stephen," she countered.

Alan, the passive and quiet CIO, was taking in the volley of words as if he were watching a tennis game

"Well, I think it's awesome," Jonathan piped up. "Nothin' like a coach to give a team some direction. It's probably like having a great director, you know?" he continued, hearkening back to his theater days as a struggling actor in New York.

Stephen gave a dismissive, "Hmph," and looked out the window.

Mitch sensed an uneasy momentum building in the room. He tried to steer himself and the team back away from what he feared could turn into the eye of a storm. "Look, let's not make more of this than it is, okay? I just wanted to inform you all that I do, indeed, have a plan of action. I think that it's a positive step. And I hope that you will, too. Here and now, I can tell you that I will keep you informed as to the steps and the progress that I'll be…making…" Mitch said, clearing his throat yet again.

"I'll be sure and take notes," Stephen said. Leslie flashed him a disapproving look.

Mitch let the stab go without comment, glancing to his notes again as he got up to address the group with what he hoped would come across as a little more authority. "The coach's name is Kate Nelson. She's very accomplished. Feel free to check out her website for more information. I do have one request of all of you."

All eyes turned to Mitch, some with enthusiasm, some with dread. *Here goes*, he thought. "I ask for your support. Kate will be calling each of you to conduct something called…a 360-Degree-Feedback." Mitch tried to hide the fact that he really had no idea what he and the team were headed for.

Maxy's cell phone rang and everyone turned to her. Mitch noticed it was the first time she'd looked enthused since the meeting began. She quickly silenced it and looked at Mitch unapologetically. Mitch felt himself falter and took his seat again.

"Whoa, whoa…wait a minute! I thought this was *your* coaching gig, Mitch," Stephen straightened his gym-toned torso for the first time. "This has nothing to do with us."

"A coach works best with a team, Steve ol' boy," Graham said. "Right, Alan?" he asked, giving him a teasing elbow that knocked his arm off the edge of his chair. Alan looked with big eyes from Graham to Mitch and nodded quickly.

Mitch glanced thankfully at Graham for the comic relief, inappropriate though it was. Bob rubbed his jaw to disguise his own smile.

Stephen was not amused. "Right, right....the consummate *teeeeeaaaaaammm* that we are."

Stephen's jab sent Mitch reeling for a few seconds. Mitch pictured himself melting down out of the seat, holding on with all of his might to the edge of the table.

"Look, let's not—" Elizabeth jumped in.

"I think that Mitch—" Leslie tried to get a word in.

"Again, please...I repeat," Mitch was annoyed with both of them for trying to speak for him. "Let's not make more of this than it is. Kate will only be contacting you to ask for your feedback on how each of you is perceiving the numbers and talent issues and my leadership. You'll have complete anonymity. I won't know who said what unless you want to tell me. It'll, it'll...." He wasn't sure exactly what it would do at this point. "It'll help give some direction. That's all."

The room was quiet. Bob looked around at the team. Mitch looked at Bob. There were tentative nods. Maxy sat up straight, sensing an end to the meeting.

Bob was the last one to file by Mitch. "This is good, Mitch. This is good."

Define 'good,' Mitch thought.

Maxy peeked her head through Mitch's door, a move that seemed out of character to Mitch. He'd never seen her look so coy, and the empathy in those big green eyes scared him. When she'd buzzed him a few minutes before, asking to speak with him, he'd made himself available. He felt himself start to get up, but was still somewhat offended by the cell phone incident during the meeting and so decided to stay seated.

"Mitch, um," she looked away for a moment and shook her head a bit, as if to get her thoughts straight before speaking. "You and I both know I haven't been happy here for a while. And, of course, there are always the rumors that fly. Well, I want to step up and be the first to let you know that I have, indeed, been recruited by another company. I'll be giving my formal resignation in writing on Monday morning."

Going on to say that she would do her best to wrap up accounts that hung in the balance and bring her direct reports up to speed to fill in the gaps until they found a replacement, Mitch knew that he was hearing only half of what she said. She finally concluded, "I have a passion for what I do, Mitch. I think that you do, too. I think that maybe the coaching will—"

He recognized the look on her face. It was the same one she'd given him during her initial interview, the look that said she needed something more substantial from him. That realization had scared him then. Now, it terrified him and it came in layers. The first layer told him that Maxy's feelings had only grown and were taking her away. The second layer told him she recognized the fact that *he* wanted something more substantial from himself, too. The third layer said that she realized he had no idea what that something was or how to reach it and that maybe the coaching *was* about more than just numbers and talent.

Mitch stood up abruptly, cutting her off. "Maxy," he said, coming around the desk, trying to take the high road of nonchalance. She got up, and he escorted her to the door. "I'm glad that you have found something suitable for you. And I really do thank you for being supportive of the coaching. You've been a great asset to us. I know you'll do well."

Closing the door behind her, he felt a tightness in his chest. His office suddenly felt very small to him, and the caffeine buzz had faded to mere jitters and inattentiveness. It was 2:30. He was hungry and tired. Leaving his coat and briefcase behind, he snatched his keys from the desktop and headed out for the rest of the afternoon.

At a stoplight a few blocks from the office he realized he didn't know where he was headed. He turned to watch some boys about his sons' ages at soccer practice. Resist though he tried, he couldn't help but think about his own countless days on the soccer field. Thinking of how easy it had been to identify offense and defense, how simple it had been to plot a strategy, he thought. *I was fearless then.* It had all started for him when his dad had rebuked his mother for letting young Mitch help her bake a surprise birthday cake for him. Mitch had heard him yell, "I didn't make it to CEO with a spatula in my hand!" Mitch had been so proud and then so crushed. It all seemed silly to him now, but after that day Mitch started spending more and more time outside, kicking the soccer ball around the yard. Mom's kitchen always smelled like coffee and home cooking and, on the days that she baked chocolate chip cookies, Mitch dribbled his soccer ball back and forth below the open window, taking it all in.

The drawn out honk of an annoyed commuter brought Mitch back to the present. He made his way down the boulevard. Before he knew it, he was wandering down the DVD section of his favorite café/bookstore with a monstrous chocolate chip cookie in one hand and a coffee in the other. The cookie was gone in no time, and Mitch, while examining the Charlie Chaplin box set he just picked up, turned the corner without paying attention.

"Mitch?!"

He almost dropped what was left of his coffee at the sound of Elizabeth's voice. Fumbling with the box set, he managed a hello. "What, uh, what are you doing here?"

"I worked through lunch. My mom's birthday is this weekend, so I came to get yet another art book for her," Elizabeth answered, actually holding several large coffee table style books. She was actually a little embarrassed, knowing that Mitch knew of her own penchant for art and loved to tease her about being a frustrated artist.

"Ah, I see. Me, too...I'm shopping for a gift, too," he lied.

"Well, mister, you're in the wrong section if you think Anna's gonna be happy with that one," she said, indicating the Chaplin set.

Mitch was completely confused and embarrassed, but it got worse when Elizabeth inadvertently reminded him of his own anniversary, which was less than two weeks away. He played it off saying that Chaplin was for the boys and he'd yet to find anything for his lovely wife.

Elizabeth always took advantage of any opportunity for Mitch's undivided attention, and he knew it. The look in her eye told him that this was one such occasion. "Mitch, I don't ask much of you. You know I'm nothing if not supportive. I'm just asking for some reciprocation. I'm not even talking about the rest of the team here. Why can't you confide more in me? I know what's at stake here more than any outside person, coach, whatever, could possibly know. One-on-one, Mitch...talk to me."

One-on-one was exactly what scared him. He'd had his fair share with Maxy already and he knew he'd have more of it than he could handle with Kate.

"Look, Elizabeth, I really can't talk about this right now. I've, I've gotta run." With that he politely excused himself, telling her they'd talk in the morning. He stashed the box set on a random shelf and set off into the early dusk.

Fear

All leaders face myriad fears: losing employees, falling stock prices, team conflict, and war and social pressures. Can you imagine how President Abraham Lincoln felt when the American Civil War broke out on April 12, 1861 as Confederate forces attacked a federal military installation at Fort Sumter in South Carolina? Do you think he was a bit afraid? I wasn't there, but my hunches tell me, "Yes...he was as scared as hell." As Abraham Lincoln once said, "*You cannot escape the responsibility of tomorrow by evading it today.*" I truly believe that, as leaders, we have to be willing to face our fears, knowing that by addressing them head on, we will become stronger and more adept at leading the people in our lives.

I believe that a company's ability to trust a leader begins with the leader's willingness to be vulnerable. It starts with the leader being willing to open up, to share his or her shortcomings and to be willing to hear feedback from team members about his or her performance and leadership capabilities. Does this dynamic feel scary for a leader? You bet it does! The approach of using a tool such as the 360 Degree Feedback Review and then talking to the team about the review process fills leaders with fear, because they know that a team of select individuals—the people who know them best—are getting ready to poke holes in the most vulnerable aspects of their lives.

Coaching Questions:

- What are you most afraid of in your life today?

- Is the fear physical, mental or emotional?

- If you actually go and address this fear, what are you concerned will happen?

- If you address this fear, how will you grow as a person?

- What type of help or support do you need in addressing this fear?

- When will you address this fear? (Name a date by which you will address this fear.)

BONUS: As a way to support you in beginning to work through your **Fear**, Roger Dewitt of Coaching NYC Inc. has provided an audio, workbook and guided imagery for readers of Edge. For more information, visit http://www.Edge-Book.com/bonus.

NINE | Avoidance

"If I were any better, I'd be twins!" Mitch said, starting off their weekly coaching call with a laugh. He went on to explain to Kate that he went with his wife to a fundraising event for The Libby Ross Foundation, her company's pet charity. Feeling that Kate had harped on the imbalance of his personal life, he was happy to be able to give himself a little pat on the back in that regard. "We were still dancing to that *Shout* song long after I'm usually in bed, so please excuse me if I seem a little tired."

"Wow, sounds like fun! No need to apologize," Kate said and then pushed Mitch to respond to the business at hand.

"As for the 360 Review, I had the meeting with my leadership team and nobody had any real qualms with talking to you, so I say let's move ahead," Mitch answered, glossing over the tension-filled discussion of five days ago.

Explaining that she'd like to actually come to the facility to conduct the interviews in person, Kate pulled yet another rug from beneath Mitch's smug stance. Mitch paused and stammered through his half-hearted agreement, thinking of Elizabeth and Stephen's resistance, not to mention his own. "I...I mean, we have our meetings over the phone. I'm curious as to why you feel the need to come here and meet with them. Though I am handsome and charming in person—" Mitch told her, with a self-deprecating snicker.

"I'm sure you are. It's beneficial for me to see you in your element, and I always try to meet my clients soon after we start working together. As a coach, I'm trained to pick up on the certain details and energy in the actual environment you and your team work in on a daily basis. I can't get that over the telephone. So, the purpose of conducting the 360 in person is twofold. First, it'll help build rapport with your team so they will be more open and willing to speak up. Second, I'll be able to see firsthand how you actually interact with them. It takes the guesswork out of the process not only for me, but for you and your team, as well. They'll see what I'm all about—that I don't have horns and a pitchfork—and that they can communicate more openly."

"Gotcha," Mitch said, pacing back and forth in his office, already wondering what Kate would see. "That means I'm gonna have to clean up my desk, doesn't it!?" Mitch said, with theatrical panic. Kate asked him, aside from minor cleaning, to leave the environment just as it normally is to let it reflect him and the way he operates in it.

Fat chance, he thought, placing his autographed Orson Welles picture in his desk drawer.

They decided on a tentative date, and then, unavoidably, the other shoe dropped. Kate brought up the manifesto. "I'd like to find out not the details of what you wrote, but how the process worked for you."

After a deep breath, Mitch launched into a long and detailed list of excuses—Anna's fundraiser, his very busy week, preparing for a presentation for a potential client—why he hadn't even touched it. "I could easily be pulled in seventeen different directions. I absolutely do not waste my time on things I do not feel are necessary...and I, I...I'm just going to be frank. I really don't understand the purpose. Again, I'm here to improve the numbers and the talent retention, and I don't see what my personal manifesto has to do with anything that happens at the office."

"What's your response about? Saying that you don't yet know what the purpose is? What's that about?" Kate responded, quite candidly.

With a hearty laugh, Mitch said, "Well, let me light some candles and incense and I'll contemplate my navel on that one."

"Fair enough. Let me ask you, is this situation just about the manifesto or are there other times in your life—personally or professionally—where someone asks you to do something, and you decide that it's not important?" Kate asked.

Mitch shared his practical perspective, that in management he finds it essential to manage time wisely and to understand the whys and project the outcomes of any task. "I'm actually proud that I don't get bogged down in minutiae," he concluded.

"Well, I understand, and you make a very good point about management skills," Kate conceded. "But we're addressing a higher level here. We're not talking about management per se...we're talking about **leadership**. I could run off twenty reasons right now why a manifesto is important and give you impressive examples of how they've worked for other leaders. I'm not going to do that, though. There's a bigger question here. That is, why are you so unwilling to take on something unless its purpose is perfectly charted and set in stone? Why are you scared to approach the unknown?"

After a long silence, Mitch finally admitted that he didn't know how to respond. The *unknown* made him think about the hazy, nebulous, awful and beautiful passions he'd avoided long ago. When he finally said, "Look, I didn't get this far by eating granola and wearing Birkenstocks," he was disturbed at hearing an echo of his father's tone in his voice.

"Well, Mitch, I'm not sure if I should let you off the hook with this one or kick you in the ass..." Kate said, catching him completely off guard. Mitch laughed, but she continued. "So let me ask you this in the meantime. I know from your client intake form that you played college soccer for a Division I team. Were you ever asked to practice your skills outside of practices or game days?"

Mitch went into a bit of a reverie, recalling how much he enjoyed honing his footwork and speed and agility. "It became almost relaxing for me, like second nature."

"And what was your coach's goal with asking you to practice these skills?"

"Well, uh, to be efficient, to be a good team player, to use your term—to kick some ass. I didn't want to let anyone down and I definitely didn't want to lose my scholarship," Mitch rattled on, saying he'd been playing soccer since he was 10.

"Mmmm. I'm getting a clear picture. So by the time you were playing for a Division I team, you knew the game inside and out, knew what would be asked and expected of you. There were no surprises, right?" Kate asked.

When he agreed, she drove home her point. "Mitch, I think that what we're dealing with right now is plain and simple. With this coaching, we're forging new ground and you haven't experienced enough of it yet to buy into it fully. You're not used to feeling that way. You're used to being very skilled at whatever you take on. Is that true?"

With some hesitation, Mitch agreed.

"I thank you for being honest about your misgivings," Kate continued, "but I ask you to do your best to have faith in this process. Remember how it felt to be in the learning curve of your earliest days of soccer."

"Well...Kate, I knew what the payoff would be in soccer. I saw it all around me. You're asking me to trust you that there will be a great payoff here, and I find that difficult to do."

"Okay...I've come to my decision. This is the point where I kick you in the ass. I am requesting that you take the time to write the manifesto and report back to me in an email—and again, you don't have to share the details of it unless you want to. Just let me know you've completed it by Monday at 5:00 p.m. eastern time."

"Okay. Okay," Mitch paused for a deep breath. "I will suspend all disbelief for the duration and do it. Expect to hear from me."

"Good. You know, this conversation has me wondering. Mitch, as a leader in the trade industry, when was the last time you took a risk that ended up paying off for you?"

"Well," Mitch paused, looking at the clock, "I'm fairly calculated in my moves. I guess, personally and professionally, I always try to minimize risk. But, I've had some payoffs," he concluded vaguely.

Pressed to consider the emotions that come into play when taking any risk, Mitch said, "...will it be worth it?...will there be a payoff?...and, even, will I survive?...you know...the skydive, the merger, the relationship."

"The big question that's looming over me, Mitch, is not if you're wondering if this crazy manifesto is going to be a waste of time...but if writing the manifesto will be risky."

"How so?" Mitch asked tersely.

"Writing the manifesto is allowing a very creative side of your life to come to the forefront, even if it's only for an hour or so."

There was a long silence on the line. Mitch's head, though, was full of rebuke from his father for checking out library books on Charlie Chaplin and Buster Keaton just a few short weeks before Dad told Mom to "sign the boy up for soccer."

"Well, that's ridiculous," Mitch finally said, "but I'll do as you ask."

"Okay. And thanks for letting me kick you in the ass," Kate said with a laugh.

Avoidance

Every day, leaders (and most people in general) find ways to avoid having to face uncomfortable situations, activities...even thoughts and feelings that seem hard to swallow. Avoidance may include a leader actually removing himself/herself from a situation, or it may involve finding creative strategies to procrastinate, delay, and avoid discussing or even thinking about what is most pressing.

Through the years of coaching hundreds of clients (and being coached myself by some of the top coaches in the world), I have learned that the situations in life that we avoid the most and feel are most risky are the areas that we **most** need to address. When tackled head on, these uncomfortable, often risky life-hurdles can provide leaders with tremendous opportunities for growth.

Coaching Questions:

- What situation are you most avoiding right now in your business or personal life?

- What is the pain/struggle/negative emotion you experience when you think about addressing this situation?

- What are you concerned will happen if you address this situation head on?

- If you address this situation head on, what will be the biggest benefit to you?

- If you continue to avoid this situation, what benefits will you receive (Example: I get to stay safe)?

- If you continue to avoid this situation, what are the potential consequences you will face?

- What are the next steps you will take to address this situation head on?

- What type of help/support do you need to address this situation?

BONUS: As a way to support you in beginning to address the topic of **Avoidance**, Kimberly George, author of *Coaching Into Greatness* has designed the EDGE Abundance Assessment. Specifically designed for leaders of today, this cutting edge assessment will raise your awareness around your current level of avoidance and resistance and will provide you with practical steps that can move anyone past their avoidance to embrace the Abundance Aptitudes of Self-Worth, Empathy, Self-Expression, Surrender, Actualization, Significance and Inquiry. The assessment is available online through this link: http://www.Edge-Book.com/bonus.

TEN | Digging

.

"So, there seems to be a change in plans," Mitch said to Bob, hoping to gain an ally.

"The only thing constant is change," he replied good-naturedly, as usual. "That's what I always say. But, what plans, specifically?"

"Well, Kate, the coach...she wants to do the 360 interviews here at the office."

"Oh, splendid! Sounds like this woman knows how to get straight down to business!" Bob said.

So much for that idea, Mitch thought. "Right!" he said, trying to cover up his disappointment. "Absolutely. So, she'll be meeting with everyone individually, and I know she wants to talk to you, too."

"Just say the word! You know I've got your back. And, Mitch," Bob looked down for a just a second, a pause just long enough to make Mitch feel both touched and uncomfortable. "...I've just got to say that I'm proud of you. You're really taking the bull by the horns here. You know, I love this company. I've done my own stint in the corporate world and I wouldn't be sitting here with you if I didn't love what I'm doing. And the qualities I see in you help to keep me inspired. I thank you for that."

Mitch swallowed the lump in his throat. He knew he should feel uplifted, but mostly he felt as if he were supporting the weight of his own heavy façade and wasn't sure how much longer he could sustain it.

On the way back to his own office, he rounded the corner and nearly ran into Graham.

"Whoa, heads up, Tiger! Hey, perfect timing! You, me. On the patio in an hour. You'll love today's lunch special!" Graham said without ever slowing. His energy never ceased to amaze Mitch. Spinning on his heels without ever missing a beat he added, "Be there!" Mitch mused that he should have been an ice skater, at least maybe a somewhat portly Disney on Ice character. *Maybe Piglet,* he thought, thankful for the slight smile he felt come over his face.

"I give you Carne D'Espeto with Piri Piri sauce!" Graham announced as Mitch joined him on the patio. Mitch inhaled and turned his face to the warm sun; it was a welcome change from the dreary weather of late. He sat down and dove in.

"This is great! One of these days, I'm gonna go with you when you visit and give my personal regards to your Mama, the original chef. Good old Cape Cod. Hell, we should scoop her up and all take a trip directly to Portugal."

"Maybe that's one trip that you and your wife could actually take *together.*" Graham said intentionally. He got *the look* from Mitch and changed the subject. "So how goes the coaching? And don't give me a pat answer; I know something's up because you haven't yet given me your usual great-but-too-much-garlic-tirade."

Mitch sat back and updated Graham on the in-person 360 interviews. "Then there's this damn...manifesto thing. She wants me to, you know, 'dig down, address my deepest desires, the things I love, my unrequited passions,'" Mitch said mockingly, making quotation marks in the air with his fingers. "I mean, I feel like I should be at some retreat in the woods, sitting in a circle and singing songs! In fact, maybe I'll call up Peter Yarrow and we could write a tune or two about my soul's journey! Together we'll bring folk music to the corporate world! It's a whole new market!" Mitch paused, and Graham just listened. "That was the part where you were supposed to laugh," Mitch said, trying to lighten it up a bit.

"I'll laugh if you say something funny. Have you told Anna about the coaching yet?"

"I'm waiting for the right time. And when it comes right down to it—here I go repeating myself **yet again**!—my personal and professional lives are distinctly separate," Mitch said, exasperated.

When Graham pushed away his plate, Mitch knew he was angry. Graham never pushed away food. "Look, Mitch, I'm not gonna pussyfoot around this issue any longer and I'm not gonna bullshit you with my witticisms, clever though they are." He leaned toward Mitch and looked him directly in the eye. "Do you know why this manifesto thing scares you?"

Mitch rolled his eyes, but heard Kate's words echoing in his head.

"It scares you because you know damn well you can't write it with your brain. You have to write it with your heart. It's like falling in love; you don't fall in love using just your brain. It takes heart and instinct. And it takes heart and instinct to create a life that you fall in love with, too, and that life includes your work. And when you do that, it shows. People respond to you before you even say a word."

The patio suddenly felt way too bright and way too warm for Mitch. And it was too quiet for way too long.

Jonathan suddenly burst through the door. "Ahhhhh, authentic home-cookin! Nice! You can always count on Graham for the real stuff!"

Mitch stirred uneasily in his chair, suddenly aware that Anna had been watching him looking at the boys through the floor to ceiling windows in the family room. She finally went upstairs, and he set down his paper and turned his attention back to his sons. It was Saturday morning, and they were kicking around the soccer ball in the yard. Again, he felt nostalgic for the confidence he'd had back in the day. The boys had it. He could see it. The longer he watched them, though, the more he realized it was more than confidence, but it was also more than he could describe. He watched them run and dribble around one another and kick in some goals. Zoe just didn't seem to understand that she'd never get her snout around that ball; her innocent tenacity made Mitch smile. The boys laughed, they stomped their feet, they yelled at each other, they pushed each other, they jumped and raised their hands in joyous victory when they scored. He sipped his coffee and tried to remember when his own emotions had run such a gamut, let alone in such a short period of time.

Anna went to run a last minute errand. Later, she was taking the boys to her parents' house for the weekend, "just to get away for a bit," she'd told Mitch. As soon as she left, Mitch ambled out to the yard. "Hey guys," he said.

"Hi, Dad," said Kyle with his 9-year old enthusiasm. Daniel gave him a nod. He was fourteen, and Mitch joked with him day by day about what was up with his dwindling vocabulary of grunts and nods. He tried to call Zoe over, but she ignored him, running back and forth between her playmates. When the ball accidentally shot his way, Mitch caught it.

As he drop-kicked it back to Kyle, he asked, "Hey, can I play?"

Without a second thought, Kyle replied, "Dad, you don't play, you watch!" and turned his attention back to his brother.

The ball may as well have hit him directly in the gut. "No, I ..." Then he realized that he had nothing to add to that statement. Kyle was right. That's exactly what he did. He watched. No more. Sometimes less. He turned and went back into the house.

Anna and the boys piled into their Volvo wagon. Mitch moved close to Anna's face and said to them all, "I love you guys." Anna put her hand on the side of his unshaven face and said, "I love you, too, Mitchell." The breathiness in her voice and the sadness in her big green eyes made his knees weaken a bit. Afraid of what she might see in his own eyes, he looked down, stepped back, and watched them pull away.

Not wanting to admit to himself that he had no idea what to do with the rest of the day, Mitch grabbed some juice from the fridge and opened up the Entertainment section of the newspaper. He caught himself tapping out a tune that was stuck in his head. He couldn't name it or even recall the lyrics, but it had been haunting him since the previous weekend. He headed to his office/den to make some headway on the pending shipping account that would hang in the balance after Maxy left.

As the sun went down, Mitch remembered the manifesto and his Monday afternoon deadline, a thought that gave him a sudden and undeniable hankering for a martini. While conceding that he'd love to write it in an absolute blackout state, he figured he'd better be clear headed. *Jeez!* he thought. *Richard Burton made a slew of films that he barely remembers and I can't allow myself one stinkin' martini over a writing assignment. I'm a dork!* he concluded, borrowing a term from Daniel's vocabulary.

Deciding he'd allow himself another indulgence, he ordered a pizza and a liter of Coke and sat down to watch Coppola's "Rumble Fish," one of his favorites. High on junk food and good cinema, Mitch was feeling pretty self-satisfied. Then, out of the blue, the rogue-ish "Motorcycle Boy," one of the main characters, said, "If you're gonna lead people, you gotta have somewhere to go." Mitch didn't even notice the next two minutes of the film. He finally clicked pause and resisted the temptation to look over both shoulders, sure to see apparitions of both Kate and Graham. *Damn it! I can't go anywhere or do anything without this leadership/coaching crap biting me in the ass!* He got up and headed to the den. *That does it! It's time!*

Mitch thought some tunes would be good in the background, but after perusing his wall of CD's, decided he didn't own any "spill your guts" theme music, so he just went with whatever was in the 5-disc changer. He turned on his laptop, but it felt too mechanical. By the time he found some notebook paper, grabbed a pen and sat there idly stroking the top of Zoe's head and recollecting conversations and events that had brought him to this point, he was at the end of a Rolling Stones CD. "Wild Horses" was one of his and Anna's favorites. He was singing it and thinking of the look in her eyes before she left and wishing he could pour some wine and take her to bed when a new CD popped on. He recognized the song instantly as the one that had been ringing in his subconscious for the last week. It was from some soundtrack that Anna had bought after a movie night with the girls. *Chick flick, chick song,* he thought. Not his style. He reached for the remote, when the lyrics themselves caught his ear.

> Staring at the blank page before you
> Open up the dirty window
> Let the sun illuminate the words that you could not find
> Reaching for something in the distance
> So close you can almost taste it
> Release your inhibitions
> Feel the rain on your skin
> No one else can feel it for you
> Only you can let it in
> No one else, no one else
> Can speak the words on your lips
> Drench yourself in words unspoken
> Live your life with arms wide open
> Today is where your book begins
> The rest is still unwritten
> I break tradition, sometimes my tries, are outside the lines
> We've been conditioned to not make mistakes, but I can't live
> that way...
> (Natasha Bedingfield, "Unwritten")

At the end of the song, the remote was still in his hand. He turned off the stereo and noticed the silence in his home. It occurred to him that he'd never really heard it before. *Where have I been?* he thought and then wondered what else he'd missed. Mitch put pen to paper and began to write words that weren't part of a business plan or communication for the first time in over twenty years.

So, I guess I'm supposed to write this as some sort of free-writing thing. Not pick up the pen, just let it flow. Well, I guess the first thing I can say is that they (has anyone ever decided who "they" are?) say your entire life flashes before you in the few fleeting seconds before you die. What if your entire life flashes before you when you're pressured into writing a manifesto, you're longing for a martini with bleu cheese stuffed olives, you've eaten an entire medium pizza by yourself (after telling yourself you'd save half for the kids), you've just drunk enough Coke to dissolve a porterhouse steak in a matter of hours, you've just been blasted by one stinking line that you never paid much attention to before in a film that you've seen half a dozen times, and some stupid pop song that your wife loves sends you reeeeeeellllling. What does that say about you? Hell if I know...

Well, okay, first to the questions that Kate presented: What pisses me off? Weak coffee. Packaged, shitty chocolate chip cookies. Call me a momma's boy, but I was spoiled! And call me old fashioned and bass-ackwards, but I sometimes wish that Anna was more of a homebody. She cooks great, healthy meals for us...with the help of our housekeeper/nanny/chef. Sometimes I feel like my home isn't even my home, you know? Sometimes I just want my wife and kids all to myself. Yeah, I'm proud of Anna and her company. She kicks ass professionally and runs this home and takes awesome care of the boys AND keeps herself in amazing shape. It's just all a little overwhelming sometimes. I'd just like things to be simpler in that arena. Every once in a while, a plate of fried chicken, bedtime for the boys, and a little more lingerie would do me just fine. Where'd that come from? I sound like my grandfather! I better change the subject. I guess other things that piss me off include closed minded, judgmental people. Hmmmm...Stephen comes to mind. That blue-blooded, manicured bore. There's gotta be more to him than that bullshit, doesn't there? What else? Ah, yes...anyone who even looks sideways at my children. I can't even go there. God, I love those boys.

What lights me up? Wow...well, creativity, music, theater, film, comedy, good wine, seamed stockings on a great pair of legs. I love my secret little forays into Chicago's comedy clubs when I'm there on business. God, if I had a sudden stroke or something and died while sitting there in the back row, Anna would wonder what the hell I'd been doing there. I think of that every single time... I love a great line from an actor in a film who knows how not to give too much away. I love to laugh. I love to make people laugh. One of these days, I wanna go to the Napa Valley Wine Auction. Visit the Coppola estate. One evening while we're there I want to go to one of the winemaker dinners...Anna and I will be dressed to kill...and did I mention the seamed stockings?...those would be for Anna, of course.

Who would I die for? No question, no hesitation. Anna and the boys. Enough said. But it would really piss me off to die. I would hate to leave this place before I do something bigger. What am I supposed to be doing? Is it this manifesto? Is it even something in this country? What will I be remembered for? Will the boys think of me as a great father? Will Anna think of me as her wonderful husband? Shouldn't I be more?

What do I stand for in the world? Jeez, I don't know. I'm no Gandhi. I'm just a guy who runs a company. And I'm funny. I'm very funny. Well maybe not VERY funny, but certainly clever and witty.

Mitch dropped the pen for a minute and cracked his knuckles, not used to writing long-hand like this. Suddenly, he was very thirsty, but decided not to let himself get distracted.

Okay, so now what? Am I supposed to write about all of those details that came in my life-that-flashed-before-me? All of those bits and pieces of memories? 45 or so years' worth? 5 pages. I have to write 5 pages. What the hell am I doing? I'm a grown man sitting alone in my den writing about my life. Aren't I just supposed to be <u>living</u> it at this point? Isn't this back-tracking just a bit???!!!! Oh, wait, that's right... I don't <u>live</u> my life; I merely "approach" it, unlike Graham, who is "actively engaged" in his life. I think that's how he put it. Arrogant bastard. No, I love the guy, but the stuff he pulls out sometimes. You don't miss a thing I say.

Hard as he tried to keep the writing flow going, Mitch couldn't help but be distracted by all of the thoughts that were connecting and firing in his mind. He recalled what Graham had said yesterday about him avoiding using his heart and instinct. He clenched his teeth for a moment but then swallowed a lump in his throat and ran his hand through his hair. He clicked the remote and listened to the song again.

I just played the song again. The last time that I listened to a song over and over and over again was after Dan died. I've never written about it before, except for that one stupid script I started and never finished. "Strong Enough." That's what I called it. Not very creative, I guess. Shit, Dan was only 16. My soccer buddy and a cinema geek, just like me. I'll never forget what his dad said to me in the hospital. "He just wasn't strong enough to survive." That really fucked with me. After the funeral, I remember, I rode my bike down to Licorice Pizza to buy the Fleetwood Mac album. Ha! Album! Vinyl! Gotta love the old skool stuff. I listened to "Say You Love Me" over and over again. It had been playing on the radio the night mom told me Dan had been in the accident. Every time I listened to it, I told myself I'd never be as weak as Dan. I'd be strong enough to survive. Maybe that means I've missed some opportunities to let my guard down every now and then. Maybe I've set myself up. Maybe now when I let my guard down people don't know who the hell I am. My wife sure doesn't. Maybe I don't even know.

This song from tonight, from Anna's CD...there's a line in it that says, "We've been conditioned not to make mistakes, but I can't live that way..." God. How many decisions have I made in my life because I was afraid of making a mistake? I don't even know. But there were some big ones. Some major decisions. Afraid of what Dad would say to me and to Mom if I didn't live up to his expectations. What, I couldn't help bake him a damned birthday cake? I was five, for god's sake! He was what?...ashamed of his boy? Well, sure. That became obvious. No impersonations allowed! Don't have any spontaneous fun, now! Don't do anything outside the realm of what Dad considers respectable, Son. I guess those weren't his actual words, but he sure as hell implied them. And I bought it hook, line, and sinker. I certainly lived up to those expectations now, didn't I!?

Mitch had forgotten how much he loved these late night hours. Writing late at night reminded him of his late teens and earliest college years, years when he was still embracing the possibilities of his own endeavors. He was on a roll. He spent another page writing about his earliest creative bents. Watching old comedies with his maternal grandfather and doing impersonations with his hats and canes.

Writing and directing plays and, as he got older, film shorts for him and the neighborhood kids—during summers while Dad was at work or away on business trips. And then there was Dad's hospitalization 10 years ago.

So I walk into the hospital room. There's my mom and my two older sisters. And there's Dad. Loopy as hell on pain meds. He opens his arms and asks for a "big old hug for your old man!" and proceeds to tell the nurse what a "goddamned creative genius" his son is. "Funny as hell, this kid!" he says and goes on to tell her about the ingenious short films I made as a kid and how I should be living in Spielberg's mansion! I didn't know he even knew about the films! Later found out Mom showed him. I was furious!!! How dare he catch me off guard like that and turn my whole perceptions of...of...I don't know...everything...upside down! I felt betrayed, I guess. God, I was a kid when I made the decisions that I thought he'd be proud of. And then he turns them around on me!?

Of course, he didn't remember anything about that incident and I'd never mention it. But what if I had gone to film school? I've still got my UCLA application in my old "Citizen Kane" script. Hilarious! Or stupid, I guess. And Rory. Whatever happened to Rory? She's probably living in LA or NY, living my dream with the open support and pride of her parents. And even if they hadn't been, knowing her, she would've had the balls to do what she wanted, anyway. Unlike me.

So where does all this put me now?...how am I supposed to keep writing when I don't know what the hell to say. I've got a wife and kids that I love, of course. I'd do anything in the world for them. Wouldn't I? And I've got a job that I also love. Or do I? I've unearthed these questions and they're sitting right out there in the bright light, just ready for examination. To what end? To what end?

Mitch got up to make that long-overdue martini. On his way to the kitchen, he let Zoe out into the backyard. He remembered the boys playing there the morning before and realized something. That gamut of emotions that he had seen in them and wondered about in himself, it was there now, sitting right there in his gut, in all of its raw pain and glory.

Digging

"Who had I become? Just another shark in a suit?"

On a corporate trip, two days after uttering these words, Jerry Maguire, who is a high profile professional sports agent in the movie *Jerry Maguire*, has a breakdown... an emotional event that paves the way for him to create a breakthrough in his life. You see, he could not escape the one simple fact: "He hated his place in the world." He had become all consumed with making money, attracting massive numbers of professional athletes as clients and losing his passion, creativity and his very self in the process.

Jerry has so much to say and no one to say it to, so what does he do? He writes a very provocative mission statement. It is not a memo, but rather 25 pages of emotionally charged ideas about what he wants for the future of his company, SMI (Sports Management International). He seizes the moment and simply writes and writes some more. When he's done, the pages are filled with memories of his passion for the sports industry, simple pleasures of his job, the sounds of the stadium when an athlete succeeds, his own dreams as a young man, what was most important in life and why he had wanted to be a sports agent in the first place.

The story of Jerry Maguire is not unlike what Mitchell James experiences in this chapter. Mitch goes through both a breakdown and a breakthrough. He cannot escape the fact that he is not satisfied with his place in his family, in the world at large or within the walls of Global Trade Management, and he begins to dig deeply into his life by writing his personal manifesto. What starts out as a struggle-laden piece of homework assigned by Kate becomes pages and pages of deeply rooted thoughts, emotions and passions about his life. He reconnects with his creativity and what was most important in life, what ticked him off, the death of his best friend, hearing the words of Graham, Kate, Anna and his father. In doing so, he opens the door to reconciling his life with them.

In coaching leaders, one of the first assignments I ask my clients to take on is to write their personal manifesto. I request that my clients take this project on with passion, that they not censor their thoughts and that they write and write until they pour the most important things about their lives onto the blank pages. Journaling is powerful and can provide leaders with a point of reconnection, a forum where they can get back in touch with what truly lights them up, what ticks them off, what they feel passionately about, what irks them and what they are willing to die for. I have discovered that, if leaders cannot take on this activity with passion and be honest with themselves about who they truly are, they usually do not grow in their leadership role.

BONUS: We invite you, as a reader of *Edge*, to start **Digging** into your personal manifesto. As a way to get you started, Andy Wibbels, author of *BLOG Wild!* has opened a private blog area for you to begin this process: http://www.Edge-book. com/bonus. As you are writing, answer the following coaching questions.

- What are you most passionate about in life?

- What are you most passionate about in business?

- What is it in life that really ticks you off?

- What is it in your business or company that really ticks you off?

- What are you most excited about in the world of leadership?

- What is it about the world of leadership that really ticks you off?

- When no one is looking, what do you love doing?

- What is something about you that most people don't know? What is it that has you keep this a secret?

- If you could start your professional life all over again, what would you be doing?

- If you could change one thing in the world, what would you change? How would you go about changing it?

- If you had $1 million to give to a cause, what would you give it to and why?

- If your life stays just as it is today, would you have any regrets? If so, what would they be?

- What do you really want for the rest of your life?

- When you are 95, and you are looking back on your life, what do you want to say was your biggest accomplishment?

ELEVEN | Feedback

Kate entered through the front door of Global with her eyes wide open. Noticing everything from the overall vibe to the smallest detail of any and every environment had become second nature to her, almost to the point of her own annoyance at times. Stopping at a new café that morning in the middle of the commute, she'd laughed at herself, thinking, *Kate Nelson, is it too much to ask to let yourself just enjoy a damned mini quiche without critiquing the "quaint but cramped" work space!* With that, she'd settled into an old wicker chair and admired the Norman Rockwell print across the tiny room.

"Nice to meet you, I'm Sue," the assistant said to Kate. "Mr. James told me to expect you..." she continued as she reached to shake hands over the top of what Kate considered a very austere, off-putting, high-top work center.

Sue tried Mitch's phone line a couple of times. "I'm sure he just stepped out of his office for a moment. Casey can escort you up," she said, indicating the other young assistant.

"Thank you, Sue. I'll find it on my own!" Kate replied, actually grateful for the chance to scope out the environment.

Kate stepped out of the elevator and continued down the hall, looking for Mitch's office. She heard a muffled greeting in the distance, followed by a distinct reply.

"So, big day. How ya' doing?" someone said.

"I am outdamnstanding, thank you very much!" another voice answered. It was loud and clear, and before she rounded the doorway, she knew exactly the source.

"Mitchell James, I presume."

Mitch stopped the flow of coffee into his mug mid-pour and spun around wide-eyed.

"Kate!" he said, turning around and adjusting his line of sight downward a good eight inches or so. He put down the carafe, quickly wiped his fingertips and shook her hand. "I'm so happy to finally meet you," he said, putting his glasses down over his eyes.

"It's wonderful to meet you, Mitch. And I know...you thought I'd be taller. I get that all the time," she said with a smile.

He quickly changed the subject. "No, no...I. Jeez. I'm sorry I missed your buzz. I just stepped out for some coffee."

From behind his back, Graham held up three fingers and silently mouthed, "Third cup." Kate smiled. Graham had been crouched in front of the fridge with a roll of paper towels and a bottle of cleaner, but he quickly stood up.

"Oh, Kate...Graham Parker. Graham, this is Kate, the coach I'm working with."

"I'm so glad to meet you. And so glad you're the one Mitch chose," he said, tossing the wad of used towels into the trash.

"It's great to meet you, too, Graham. Not cleaning on my account, I hope," she said teasingly. She was used to this sort of scramble that her imminent arrival always caused.

"Ah, I see I am transparent, as always," Graham said with a consensual and playful bow of his head.

Kate laughed and liked him already. She took Mitch up on his offer of some coffee while he explained the evolution behind Elizabeth's Special Brew. Kate instantly felt a certain staff camaraderie as she watched the stream of java waver its way into the mug. Mitch's hand shook slightly, and she noted it.

"Well, shall we?" she asked.

"Yes, yes. By all means," said Mitch, taking a step back to allow her through the door before him. As she turned through the threshold, she heard Mitch say softly, "See you on the hotseat!" to which Graham replied, "You *are* outdamnstanding, by the way. Don't forget it!" She smiled to herself.

In the office, Mitch tried to steer her toward a chair, but she was in no hurry. "Welcome to my world," she heard him say, and took note of the tone of mock grandeur.

She nodded and headed toward the expanse of the windows. "You've got a great space here, Mitch. Lots of potential."

Mitch didn't reply, but she saw him give a slight nod before taking another big gulp of coffee. She figured the word *potential* was probably anathema to him. She intentionally let the silence fall where it may and was glad when Mitch joined her at the window. "Yeah, I love the view from here. During a crazy day, this view is kind of a saving grace," he said without looking at her.

"How so?" she asked.

"Well...perspective, I guess. You know, like I said. I don't like the minutiae-kinds-of-things. Looking out this window down on the city and toward the river and beyond reminds me to keep my focus big...wide."

She thought the view was about the only thing that felt big and wide in the office. Everything else was old school, dark wood, somewhat cluttered. Feeling the need to reign Mitch's focus back in a bit, she asked him to take a seat with her and continued, "Mitch, I want to thank you for proceeding with this 360 Degree Interview Process. I assure you, I will do my best to keep things very straightforward. Like I said, at every turn, I proceed with the assumption that you are already one of the best of the best."

"Thank you. Thank you, I do appreciate your stance, Kate."

There they were, the entire team, ready to proceed. Kate watched Mitch survey the group with both pride and trepidation. His gaze was interrupted by a sudden blink and look of surprise when he noticed the attractive brunette in the room; Kate couldn't help but wonder what that was all about but had to smile when she saw the supportive looks on most of the other faces.

She thanked Mitch for his kind introduction and explained the 360 Process to the group, revealing that each of them would be asked to rate Mitch on a scale from 1-5 in twelve areas of competency. Kate assured everyone of their confidentiality and thanked them all for their participation, saying that after she and Mitch took a brief tour of the facility—so that she could get a feel for the space—she'd spend the balance of the day meeting with them one by one for at least 45 minutes each. Jonathan was the first to write his name on Kate's list.

"Jonathan, I see that you believe in Mitch wholeheartedly, but I want to go back and touch on something. I asked you about the third competency, Offers employees challenging learning situations, specifically to build skills and produce bottom line results. You ranked Mitch with a four but then when we started talking about Mitch's creativity in the business, you went back and changed it to a five. What's that about?"

Jonathan paused. "Sharp cookie," he said. "Kate, I love the guy. I guess I'm more loyal than I even realized. I know that this is all confidential, so I wouldn't want this to get back to Mitch, of course..." He shifted in his chair. "I love my job. It's not perfect, but I'm happy. I feel challenged just by the nature of this business and its scope. Me? I'm a self-starter. I like to create my own challenges. So, it's not *my* issue. But I can't ignore the gossip and the grumblings. As far as the creativity issue goes, sure, there are times when I'd like Mitch to come to me with some creative, edgy challenge to bring up the numbers. So...you got me. I guess that's why I changed my answer. The bottom line is, I guess I'm a little protective of Mitch."

Kate let Jonathan sit with that statement for a few moments. "So, how would his being more creative help you in your job?" she asked.

"Well...in sales...business in general...you can't do it right if you're not creative. I don't know. I can't put my finger on it, but I just feel like there's stuff there in Mitch just beneath the surface. It's like he's not really even aware of what people see in him. Does that make sense?"

"Absolutely."

"Good, 'cause I know I can sometimes come across like I'm full of shit, but in this case, I don't think I'm—oh, sorry..." he caught himself.

"No, please. I like people to be candid," she assured him. "While we're being candid, I've got to say that I *love* the beanbag chair!"

"Oh, yeah. I can't brainstorm on creative sales ideas behind a desk. That thing's as essential as my computer! That's the hotspot of my office!" he said with a proud nod.

"I like your style."

"Well, Mitch hates it...but Graham loves it. He tells Mitch he's gonna get one to match mine. We're even considering lava lamps. *Shhh...don't tell Mitch!*" Jonathan said with raised eyebrows, getting another laugh out of Kate. "You know, you're a lot more hip than I thought you'd be."

"Really? What did you think I'd be?" she asked.

"Oh, I don't know...maybe older, more traditional, like a therapist friend of my mother or something."

"Well, I'm happy to exceed your expectations! And what are you selling?... 'Cause I'll take a dozen! But first I want to hear more on what you were saying on the subject of creativity," Kate said, getting back to business.

"Cool," he said, sitting back with a big grin. "Well, I spent some time doing theater and never thought I'd find a fit in the corporate world, but here I am, and Mitch helps make this a great gig. In fact, Mitch reminds me of people I knew in the theater world."

"Theater? Yeah, I can see that in you," Kate said and left it at that, not wanting to give away her own vague intuitions about Mitch's latent creativity.

"I think the guy is more creative than he lets on," Jonathan continued. "I'd like to see that side of him more. He's polished, but I'd like to see some edge, you know. I think he should buck the Board more than he does. I don't know... Mitch seems like he is a very creative, open leader, but he leads like he's old school...and I just don't get that about him...like he's trying to lead like Bob might lead. Like he's wearing a suit that's too small for him but thinking that he looks really good. The sad part is that everyone else notices the bad fit and makes fun of him."

He stopped and rubbed his jaw, looking uncomfortable.

"It's okay. You're not betraying confidences here, Jonathan. Mitch is participating in this process because he *wants* to make changes. Your honesty is helping him."

He nodded. "I guess I was just thinking that, as an actor—former actor, I guess—I see these kinds of things. Human nature, you know?" he said, leaning forward again.

Kate loved how easy he was to talk to. His Matthew McConaughey charm and looks didn't hurt, either. They moved through the remaining competencies.

"Just one more," she said. "How would you rank Mitch on **Leads with an authentic leadership style**?

Jonathan sat back and smiled.

"Why are you smiling? What does that mean?" Kate asked.

"I'm actually smiling because I'm uncomfortable answering that question."

Try as she may, Kate couldn't seem to get comfortable herself in the next office. "Elizabeth, how would you rank Mitch on this competency: **Takes reasonable risks in order to improve the company.**"

"A three, I guess," she replied without hesitation.

"Okay, **Looks at situations from multiple viewpoints in order to gain perspective.**"

"Can I say three and a half?"

"Sure," Kate returned. She'd seen these kinds of terse responses before. It all made sense considering that Elizabeth sat across the desk from her with her arms crossed over a plain gray suit. What Kate couldn't reconcile, though, was the stark contrast between Elizabeth's standoffish nature and the vibrant urban and African-American art that covered the walls. She pressed on. "And *Offers employees challenging learning situations, specifically to build skills and produce bottom line results.*"

"Oh, a three, I guess."

"Alright. And *Develops trust with the team.*"

"Between two and three. Two and a half," Elizabeth said without breaking her stride.

"Very well. Let me ask you about these scores, Elizabeth. Are you someone who just doesn't give high scores in general, or do these numbers reflect your actual feelings?"

Elizabeth took a visible breath for the first time since Kate had entered the room. "Look, I just don't get this," she said. "It doesn't make sense. I see Mitch in action around here every day. I know he's got work to do; everyone knows it." She finally uncrossed her arms and continued. "But I also know how competent he is!"

Kate sat back and gave her room.

"There's something missing in this whole equation, but...look, no offense, but Mitch is looking in the wrong place to find it."

"What do you mean?" Kate asked.

"I am the COO of this company. In plain and simple terms, that title means that I am second-in-command. But you'd think that Graham was second-in-command. Mitch turns to him for everything! I know they're friends, but on a professional level, it's inappropriate. And then there's this..." Elizabeth paused.

"Go ahead. Please be candid," Kate said.

"It's this coaching thing. If Mitch relied more on the team, and more on me, we wouldn't be in this position."

"Tell me how you envision your professional relationship with Mitch," Kate said.

Elizabeth explained the business model she'd read about in a leadership journal, wherein two leaders were at the helm of the company, each accountable to the other in any and all decision making. "But because Mitch is so competent, he doesn't rely on or ask the rest of us for enough. He slits his own throat. He should ask for more from the team. And I have to add that none of us appreciate it when Mitch occasionally *vanishes* on a Friday afternoon without telling anyone where he is going. It's as if he thinks he's entitled to skip out and that we don't notice when he just leaves at 3:00 without any mention of anything...and then I run into him at...oh, never mind."

As Elizabeth continued, Kate was fascinated by the dichotomy of her obvious creative side and its sharp contrast to her defensive business style. *Two peas in a pod,* she thought, thinking of Mitch. *Some mirroring going on here.* With feedback from only two of the team so far, Kate was sensing the nuts and bolts flying off of this not-so-well-oiled machine.

"Wow, I'm exceeding my coffee quota for the day, but pour on..." Kate said, as Leslie got up to refill her coffee mug.

"We have such great coffee here, you know," Leslie said. "Anyway, could you repeat that last one?"

"Sure," Kate replied. ***"Demonstrates competence and credibility in his area of expertise."***

"Oh, a five plus!" Leslie said, returning to her seat next to Kate with a big smile. "You know, Mitch really is the best boss I've ever had. So poised and confident. It makes us so proud to know that he's sought out so often for his advice in this business."

Kate took notes feverishly. She'd seen this dynamic before and noticed how frequently Leslie used the word *we*, speaking for the entire team whenever possible. As the head of HR, Leslie was the nurturer here, the sort of mother hen protecting the leader of her brood at every turn. Kate couldn't help but think of her son's kindergarten teacher back in the day.

"How about **Attracts and retains top talent**."

Leslie's expression changed completely. The perky grin was gone. After a few seconds, she bit her lip. "A two, I guess, maybe a three. I don't know."

"Can you explain that score?"

"Well, I don't want to betray Mitch." Leslie sighed deeply. "I guess we all sort of protect him from hearing any bad news. So, it's hard to communicate some-times...but I'll tell you, Kate, as head of HR, we keep losing great people. Our top players are saying that they are not challenged enough. I feel like we are losing our stronghold in the market because we keep losing great talent to our competitors."

Leslie stalled, looking like she felt she'd said too much. "I feel like I should remind you that anything you say to me is confidential," Kate mentioned.

"Right," Leslie replied, straightening her shoulders a bit. "You know, Global has always had a great reputation for attracting A-players. I love that! In fact, I'm a big fan of Bradford Smart's book, *Top Grading*. Have you heard of it?"

Kate started to respond, but Leslie was on a roll. "It's all about that dynamic of attracting the best of the best. I recommended it to Mitch, but I doubt he ever read it. Anyway, we attract excellent people with the promise of creative, challenging environments and unlimited growth potential in every department...and then we don't deliver. People get bored and then they leave. It's very frustrating. I feel stagnant because the whole dynamic limits me in my job, too. I feel like I am in a revolving door, constantly having to hire and acclimate new talent. Not to mention how expensive it is to hire and train new people."

"Well, that leads me to wonder how you feel about the next competency. **Leads with an authentic leadership style**," Kate continued.

"Well, jeez, I hope I'm not saying too much. I read all the time, and that book and some other articles I've read in business journals mention *authentic leadership*. They all had me wondering about Mitch...if he is really leading from a place that is *authentic*. I don't know how to say this, but I've never felt that Mitch has really shown us his true side. I mean, he tells the truth...he's honest and a straight shooter, but I get the feeling that we don't get to experience all of Mitch at the office.... like he leaves a part of himself out of this company. And I do hear people say those kinds of things quite often in exit interviews. People say that they thought they were being hired by a very dynamic, creative leader, and they leave because they feel let down by Mitch. I don't know. Does that make sense?"

"Yes," Kate said.

"Good," Leslie continued and then paused.

"What would change that feeling for you?" Kate asked.

"I don't think any of it can change without Mitch changing."

Well into his conversation with Kate, Stephen interrupted his own train of thought. "Look, I think that—overall—Mitch is a good guy, and I wouldn't be here if I didn't. I don't work for anyone who is not competent...and you can quote me on that!"

Kate smiled and nodded, seeing right through Stephen's steely demeanor. "Well then, what do you think of this competency: *makes decisions that might be unpopular if it is in the best interest of the customer*?"

"Well, I'd say three point five, maybe four. Mitch could take some more stands and make some decisions that might seem unpopular in order to grow this company. He could stretch a little more to inspire the customers. They do provide the bottom line for us, after all," Stephen said.

"Got it," Kate said. And for the CFO, it was apparently all about the bottom line and its growth. "So, how does that idea tie into how he *thinks about company growth and explores new ideas for organizational development?*"

"I'd say about a three. Frankly, this place is boring. If people could focus less on gossip and idle talk and more on moving the numbers, the growth would be inherent. It would just happen. Period. And Mitch has the potential to make that happen," Stephen concluded, cracking his knuckles.

Kate was momentarily distracted when she noticed that the quality of his manicure rivaled hers. She stumbled her way into the next question.

"*Looks for new ways to achieve a competitive advantage in current business practices.*"

"Maybe three and a half again. I'm here because I know this company's track record, and I know its potential. But, if the numbers don't improve, and I'm not allowed the freedom to push 'em forward, then, I don't know. Losing A-players is expensive, you know. And we're losin' 'em left and right. When they leave, they take knowledge with them. It's a vicious cycle." He paused for a moment. "I really think that Mitch knows he could do better...and I think that he probably beats himself up a lot about it. And that's too bad," Stephen said, as his left eye crinkled ever so slightly at the corner.

"Hmm…" was all she said for the moment, wondering about the chink she'd just seen in his armor. "And how well *could* he do?"

"I don't know. I mean that's up to him, right?" he said, sitting up straighter. "He has the potential to be the top leader in this industry, but he seems to be choosing to play it safe. No one hands you anything in this life. You make your mistakes, you pay for them. You do well, people like you. Plain and simple." He crossed his arms and cocked his head in a way that told Kate he had nothing more to say on the subject.

Kate made a few more comments on the form and understood why this man was CFO. Rows and columns, black and white…with just a smidgen of room for the occasional shade of gray that made him interesting.

"Thank you, Stephen. I appreciate your time."

He nodded. As she got up to leave the office, she felt his eyes on her legs and smiled to herself with the wisdom of her youthful 49 years.

Alan greeted Kate awkwardly with a nod of his head, instantly endearing himself to her. She noted just a hint of a lingering Japanese accent. They took seats in chairs that Kate thought were rather uncomfortable and not at all conducive to productivity. *High tech meets 1980 cubicle.* He kept adjusting his glasses as if he wasn't sure what to expect, and when she noted Alan clearing his throat and pushing back the cuticles on his bitten nails, she knew that it was time to move along with the questions.

"Oh, Mitch is the smartest man I know!" Alan replied when she asked how he felt about his boss and his level of competence.

"Really? Tell me more about that," she urged.

"Well, he can go with the flow when he needs to, but pretty much he keeps things sort of...you know, stable. Stability like that makes people feel comfortable."

Kate wondered how Alan would do with the changes that were afoot.

"No, we don't experience much change around here. It's pretty predictable from day to day." The big smile on his face told Kate that he liked it that way.

He didn't have any opinions to offer on creative leadership, and when Kate asked him if Mitch knew how to think outside the box, he asked, "What box?"

"Let me rephrase that. Would you consider Mitch an agent for change in order to grow the company?"

"Umm...I don't know. Too much change means you're still looking for what's right for you. Mitch is solid." As if by default, Alan turned back to his computer and clicked his monitor back to life.

With that, Kate thanked him with a smile and let the Corporate Information Officer return to life as he knew it within the safety of his office's four walls. As she glanced down at her watch, she realized that Alan had just set a 360- interview-land-speed-record.

"I'm not sure that I'm the best person for you to be talking to," Maxy said as she and Kate settled into adjacent chairs.

"Why is that?"

"Do you not know that I'm leaving?" Maxy answered with a tilt of her head.

"Oh, you're leaving?" Kate asked, surprised.

"Well, yes...I just assumed that Mitch had probably told you..." she answered. Kate thought she sounded a little disappointed, but wasn't sure if it was because she was leaving or because Mitch hadn't made mention of her exit.

"No, he didn't, but this situation is all the more reason for me to be talking to you. I just ask that you be very candid," Kate said.

"Yeah, I guess there's no reason not to be, right?" Maxy said with a shrug.

"True. I'll just go through the competencies, and you let me know what you think," Kate replied. *"Takes reasonable risks in order to improve the company."*

"Two. I don't think that Mitch remembers how to take a risk," Maxy said.

"Looks at situations from multiple viewpoints in order to gain perspective."

"Well, sure. A four, I guess. But actions speak louder than words. He *looks* at situations but doesn't act on his insights."

"Offers employees challenging learning situations, specifically to build skills and produce bottom line results."

"I have to give him a two on that one. I was promised those sorts of challenges...but they never materialized."

"Develops trust with employees and team."

"Two. Again, I'd say he's a trustworthy person on a personal level, but on a professional level, my trust for Mitch is pretty much gone. He didn't deliver the challenges and growth opportunities he promised, and he didn't allow me the freedom to create them myself," Maxy said, shaking her head.

"Displays confidence when presenting ideas or expressing opinions to others."

"Absolutely. I'll give him a four and a half there. That's one of the things that endeared this company and Mitch to me. Mitch comes off as very confident. He could have you believe just about anything. You'd think the guy was an actor or something!"

"Listens carefully to others to understand their needs and concerns."

"A three. No more than a three. Sure, he always seemed to be empathetically listening every time I asked for more challenge. But no follow through."

"Makes decisions that might be unpopular if it is in the best interest of the customer."

"That question's unfortunately almost laughable. There've been plenty of times when I've questioned in whose best interest Mitch is acting. Dare I say, it's usually been the Board's best interest...or at least what Mitch perceives to be his best interest in light of what he feels the Board wants. I don't think that it's selfish or malicious or even intentional. I think that it probably just feels safe for Mitch to do what he thinks is expected of him...almost like a kid who's trying to please someone. Gosh, I hope I'm not out of line..."

"Not at all," Kate said. "I appreciate your openness. How about this one? *Looks for new ways to achieve a competitive advantage in current business practices.*"

"A two. Mitch totally loses sight of the competitive advantage! I'm a very competitive person. That's why I'm leaving...and I'm leaving for Global's biggest competitor because they've spelled out in spades exactly what kind of competitive edge I'll be encouraged to create. And it's not about the money. I won't be making more than I am now right off the bat. But I will be allowed and encouraged to create an environment with unlimited growth potential in all areas. That's exciting. And that's what people want. Or at least it's what I want."

"Attracts and retains top talent."

"Well, he's got the first part of the equation...but not the second part. I'll give him a one point five. He's got the substance there beneath all of the nice, shiny, attractive things that draw people to him. He needs to peel back whatever it is that's covering it all up! That's the good stuff. I hope he can get to it somehow."

"*Leads with an authentic leadership style*."

Maxy paused and shook her head. "I'd still be here 100% if he did."

Sitting in the oversized chairs in Bob's office, Kate thought of herself as Rita Moreno playing the little girl in "The Electric Company" skits. All she needed was a big lollipop and pigtails. Sitting up as straight as possible, she moved to the edge of the chair to take notes more comfortably.

Bob poured himself a fresh cup of coffee from his thermal carafe while explaining how his love for this company and his faith in Mitch were the only things keeping him from full-fledged retirement and more time in the South Pacific. Kate could see why this man inspired so much respect in Mitch.

"May I see your list of competencies there?" Bob asked, sitting next to her.

She handed him the list, and he quickly looked it over. "Well, I've got to say that I'll give Mitch a four on most of these. On **Demonstrates competence and credibility in his area of expertise**, I'll go with a five; Mitch's competence has had me on his side for years, long before he came to this company. On **Attracts and retains top talent** I'll go with a three. That's where you come in," he said with a smile. "The Board, frankly, is breathing down my neck about our numbers and our talent loss. We need to gain their approval again. You're going to help my boy reach fives on all of these, right?"

"That's why I'm here," Kate said.

"Look, Ms. Nelson..."

"Kate. Please call me Kate," she said, hoping not to offend his sensibilities.

"Very well. Kate it is," and he raised his coffee mug. "I won't pretend to know what this whole coaching movement is all about. I mean, I've heard great things about it at a few conferences. I've done my research. I'm no dinosaur, and I don't want this company to follow in their footsteps and end up on the extinct list. As you can imagine, I'm pretty old school, but that doesn't mean I can't open up a bit. I believe in my CEO. I was instrumental in getting him in here in the first place. He has chances that I never had as a man his age. I want to help him take those opportunities. I know that he can build a team and retain it, grow it."

"Bob...what do you want to happen as a result of the coaching?"

"I think that Mitchell James is one of the most competent, inspirational leaders I know, but there is something missing from the equation. I am feeling as if I have a superstar who has decided to play a mediocre game. What I know he is capable of achieving is not matching up with what he is actually doing. It's as if he intentionally holds himself in a place that is safe. I want to see him take more risks. I want to see him get in there and make this team into a superstar team. Mitch needs to step up his game."

"Well," Graham said, "I'm a big fan of personal growth and accountability. For that very reason, your client and I share a sort of love/hate relationship."

"Well, perfect! Then you and I will get along famously!" she said, and they both laughed. "Very functional office space," Kate noted, looking around the room and nodding.

"Thank you, ma'am! I do my best with the Feng Shui thing, you know. Well, as well as I can do in this brick and mortar building!" Graham said, rolling his eyes.

"What do the rolling eyes mean?" Kate asked, catching Graham off guard.

"Oh, you got me. I'm usually the one to catch those innuendos. Well, surely you can tell that I'm not exactly an old-school kind of guy. The brick and mortar thing is just not free enough for me...and it doesn't suit Mitch either...or this company! We need room to breathe and grow freely!"

"Well, in that vein, what do you think of Mitch in relation to this competency: *Takes reasonable risks in order to improve the company?*" she asked.

"Mitch definitely needs to break the mold he's created for himself. A three. I give him a mere three," Graham answered.

Going on to assure Kate that he backed her efforts 100% and would be there to give Mitch a swift kick in her stead if necessary, Graham reinforced her opinions of Mitch's latent creative side. "I see a side of Mitch that many people don't see during work...he has a fun, light-hearted style that we could really use here, and we don't see it. But I know for a fact that it's there."

"Interesting that you say that. I wanted to ask you if you think that Mitch **leads with an authentic leadership style**."

A big smile spread across his face. "Well, let me tell you a little something. Sure, he gives me a hard time about all of the workshops and authentic empower-ment things that I do, but he keeps coming back for more advice. I know that if—deep inside—he weren't just achin' to bust out with a slap-happy-pappy of his own, we wouldn't be the close consistent friends that we are!"

"Wait...a slap...what?" Kate asked, already smiling at Graham's enthusiasm.

"A slap-happy-pappy! Girl, don't tell me you've never seen a slap-happy-pappy!" He jumped up and did a comical double handed ham-bone, blues kind of rhythm beat on his thigh that absolutely broke Kate up.

"That's hilarious!" she said, and couldn't stop laughing.

"I saw him do that *one time*! One time, Kate." He sat back down next to her. "It was during a barbeque, some big friends and family thing he and his wife had. Lots of adults and kids. He and his kids—and everyone else's—were dancing around in the backyard, and he broke out with that. The kids loved it and followed him around for an hour! That silly stupid inspiring little dance," he said, "is a metaphor for what I'd love to see more of in Mitch...I just want to see him step into himself. Aside from what the Board wants, doing so would meet and exceed his **own** expectations, his own authentic style!"

"Well said, Graham. Well said," Kate concluded with a smile.

"Hey, one question...off the record. Did you notice the autographed Orson Welles photograph in his office?"

"Orson Welles? No...but—off the record—your question doesn't surprise me," Kate said with a nod and an even bigger smile.

Mitch had a restless afternoon and a nearly sleepless night. He had one dream that lasted all night long, in an endless loop of abject terror. In fits of sleep, he dreamed that he was back in college as a double major in international business and film. Lost in indecision, he hadn't attended a single class all quarter, but had spent what seemed like an eternity wandering aimlessly around the campus. By the quarter's end, he looked like a homeless person. The dream culminated in final-exam day, and Mitch was but a caricature of himself running frantically back and forth between the two departments, never finding the right classrooms and knowing that even if he had, he'd have been a grossly unprepared idiot. *Why am I rehashing this crap?* he thought when he awoke.

When he got to the office, there it was, as expected. In the slew of emails sat the one from Kate with the subject line "360 Results." Mitch decided to top off his nearly full coffee mug before diving in and calling Kate for their appointment. After a few hearty swigs of java, he opened the email. By the time he'd read just the first few lines, he was reeling. With the form staring at him relentlessly from the screen, he set his jaw and punched in the numbers on the phone like a man on a mission.

"So, I sense a bit of sarcasm about the 360. To backtrack, I commend you for completing the manifesto, but before we go there, would you like to discuss the interviews?" Kate asked.

"Yeah, Kate, let's do that. I seem to have something stuck in my craw that I just can't get around...Look, I'm just gonna be brutal here. I think it's a crock of shit! Excuse me for being frank. I'm actually a little annoyed...actually shocked and quite pissed. Um, I don't know what to do with this. It feels awfully touchy-feely to me and way off base. I'm scrolling up and down here...*I feel like Mitch leads based on what was done before...want to see him step into his own leadership style*...and the comments about people not knowing when I leave the building early on Fridays. That's ridiculous! I don't understand that. I am incredibly honest and upfront, and I always tell people when I am leaving the building. If I knew who said that, I'd probably have a much better perspective...I could put it in context. Who said this crap about not being challenged? I bet that was Maxy. Was it?"

"Well, Mitch, let me remind you that, because of confidentiality, I'm not at liberty to divulge who said what. And I hear this response quite often when I debrief a 360...people always want to be able to attach certain comments to certain people because it's easier to make sense of it all and even to dismiss certain things. I can tell you, though, that the idea of you leading authentically came up in almost every conversation I had. Your team perceives you as honest and speaking the truth. They're just not sure they've seen your true side as a leader."

"What!?" Mitch was incredulous.

When Kate took a step back and asked him what part of the results he'd like to explore first, he said that anything with a 4.5 or better was okay. It was the other sections that disturbed him.

"Well, some of these things...jeez, lead *authentically*...that's just bizarre. Anyway, *more creative outlets*...what, am I supposed to bring in a string quartet and instruments for everyone? We're talking business here! And challenging talent, well, sure, that's part of why I'm working with you. But they need to bring something to the table, too. A *more fun environment*...Well, great, I'll put a slide in the break room and we'll all take turns! You know, I wanna know who said they're *bored*, 'cause I'll change that real quick!" Mitch paused for a breath.

"Let me tell you something, Mitch. I went through my own 360 about a year ago, and I felt just like you. I was angry. I wanted to know who said what and why. But after sitting with the information for a week or more, I realized that, as a leader, the perceptions of those I am leading are my reality. That's not to say that they're all necessarily *right*, but those perceptions are what I have to address."

Mitch was quiet for a few moments. "Perception is everything, I suppose."

"Okay, so let me ask you what's important about knowing about the perceptions of those you lead," Kate pressed.

Mitch pondered a bit, even repeating the question to himself. "Well, sure, those perceptions are mirrors of sorts, I guess, but I feel like the bottom line is a much better indicator of your performance. Can't we all just be adults here, put aside these little things, and do our *jobs?* I am, frankly, an incredible driving force in this business. This authenticity thing feels like a slap to my integrity! I am an honest, upfront man."

Reading from the 360 form itself, Kate reminded him of how much his team expressed trust in him and regarded him with honesty. Mitch was puzzled. She asked him to consider the distinctions between honesty and leading authentically.

"Honesty is based in truth and clarity, no lies. It seems black and white, absolute. Authenticity...hmm...Well, I could go to an art museum and believe that a painting is an authentic piece, when really it's a knockoff. So, authenticity is based largely on the perceptions of the beholder...or the ones being led...and they can be wrong."

"Sure, I'll give you that. But let me draw another analogy with art. Many times, artists—painters, film directors—start their work by imitating the masters and then steadily bring in their own nuances of style. Well, your team said that they feel you lead based on what other leaders have done. They want to see your own style... and they seem to know that there's more to you than they can put their fingers on. They want to see more of the bigger, bolder, more out-there Mitch that you've only allowed them glimpses of."

"Interesting," Mitch replied. While he said that he was still waiting for clarity on the big picture of the 360 results, he conceded that what Kate had said about copying a master makes sense. "The replication of something is to create technique. To be a master, you make that technique your own."

"Well said! And your team sees you as a master of the hard and fast leadership skills. Now they want you to take them higher. They want you to inspire them! So, I ask you this, Mitch," Kate continued. "What part of yourself, of your own technique, are you leaving outside of the workplace?"

Mitch stuttered and stammered, finally saying, "I'm not leaving out anything that's not appropriate."

"How do you know what's appropriate?"

"Well, I guess what's appropriate is what the team wants, but according to the 360, my team protects me, so how would I even know what they want?" Mitch countered. Hemming and hawing some more, he finally said, "Well, I suppose there is something. I say this with the caveat that I don't know how or if this information applies, but...in my manifesto...I did see a glimpse of my creative side that I just sort of...well, I just don't really go there any more. Again, I don't know how that side of me would ever apply to work."

Kate explained that she didn't know either, but went on to say that she worked with two kinds of people: people who took the results of their 360, addressed them, implemented them, and saw great change in their business and in their lives in general...and those who didn't. She also shared the story of Decision Tech, one of their major competitors. "Following their own 360 in 2000, there were a lot of grumblings and gripes, so the CEO decided to go public with the information, going so far as to do interviews with *Business Week* and *Fortune*. Obviously, they addressed the changes that their team wanted in a big way, even going so far as to redesign the physical environment. The results were astounding, as you can see by their success. So, I ask you this: I'm not telling you to divulge of yourself in this way, but I am asking you, what are you willing to do with your results?"

"Well, surely, as painful as it is, there is something to it. And just as I was with the manifesto, I'm willing to look at this and consider breaking new ground." With some powerful questioning from Kate, Mitch decided that the next step was to circulate the 360 results, address the team and let them be heard. "I guess I need to give them permission not to protect me. To be honest with me."

Kate remained silent...to let this thought sit with Mitch. She then reminded him that there was a fine line between being authentic and totally compromising yourself to be exactly what others expect of you. "Let me make a clear point. Your team doesn't want to mold you, either. They simply like the 'real you' they've seen mere glimpses of and want to see more."

"Yeah, well, I guess it's my default to focus on the negative, to think that they're saying that I need to be **fixed**."

Kate explained that that was a common phenomenon with high achievers, with people already in leadership positions. "Just remember, Mitch, that you already have skills like trust and communication securely in place. Your team regards you as highly competent. So, when we talk about *leading authentically*, we're talking about an entirely different level...becoming the cream of the crop."

"You mean an *uber leader*!" Mitch said with a German accent.

"Exactly! It's about transparency—warts and all—where your actions will speak as loudly as your words." She went on to remind him, however, that leaders walk a fine line between being authentic and maintaining authority. "This is not to suggest that you will go into the office every day and use your team for a therapy session!" she said with a laugh.

"And I don't have to lead them in folk songs?!"

"No, unless you all decide you want to do that. And the good thing is, the cat is out of the bag. Your team no longer has to protect you and talk behind your back. They have told me how they feel, and I am the messenger," Kate said. "And, speaking of the team...you mentioned the *creative* person that surfaced a bit in your manifesto. When you talk with them about the 360 results, I have a request. I would like for you to observe this new conversation as part of a new *creative* process. Let yourself see what is created in that dialogue as a starting point for breaking new ground. Does that make sense?"

"Hmm...that's an interesting perspective. I'm surprised to hear myself say that, yes, it does. I'll consider that. Interesting...After they let me know...I'll guess I'll let you know..."

Feedback

As an Executive Coach, I conduct at least twenty 360 Degree Feedback reviews every year. I have found that one of the best approaches is the face-to-face interview with both team and board members and even family members when possible.

If I were to come into your life and talk to 8-10 people who know you best, on a scale of 1-5, with 5 being the highest, how would they rank you in the following areas?

- Takes reasonable risks in order to improve the company;

- Looks at situations from multiple viewpoints in order to gain perspective;

- Offers employees challenging learning situations, specifically to build skills and produce bottom line results;

- Develops trust with employees;

- Communicates openly and honestly;

- Displays confidence when presenting ideas or expressing opinions to others;

- Listens carefully to others to understand their needs and concerns;

- Makes decisions that might be unpopular if it is in the best interest of the customer;

- Thinks about company growth and explores new ideas for organizational development;

- Looks for new ways to achieve a competitive advantage in current business practices;

- Demonstrates competence and credibility in his or her area of expertise;

- Attracts and retains top talent; and

- Leads with an authentic leadership style.

TWELVE | Vulnerability

Walking to the conference room, Mitch's frantic college exam nightmare kept running through his head. Just steps away from the door, he took a u-turn and headed to the restroom. He stood there and looked at himself in the mirror for a minute. He forced out a quick breath and noticed the fine lines around his eyes. Squinting a bit for exaggeration, he decided that they weren't so bad for an oldish guy. He threw his shoulders back, cocking his head and rehearsing his stance. "Okay, lookin' good. Feelin' good. Ready for some changes..." he was rattling on beneath his breath. "Great! Six months ago I had my shit together. Now I'm standing next to a urinal talking to my reflection." *I don't know what I'm doing, but I used to have a master plan!* he thought. Rubbing his hands together and flashing back to a million episodes of Scooby Doo, he shot back at the man in the mirror with one of his favorite impressions, "And I would've gotten away with it, too, if it hadn't been for you meddling kids!" He rubbed his face and gave his reflection an affirmative nod that said it was time to face the music. Then he shook his head. "Who am I kidding?" he said aloud, dropping his head and heading out the door.

With an un-firm grip, Mitch turned the knob and entered the conference room with his head held high, but not convincingly so. "Good morning, everyone!" They all responded tentatively, Leslie's voice ringing above the group. Wasting no time with small talk, he sat at the head of the table.

"Thank you. I want to thank you all for your participation yesterday in the 360 process. I know that it was something new for all of us. It was certainly new for me..." Mitch got distracted for a moment by the sympathetic look on Leslie's face, which was quickly countered by a wink from Graham. "But we're all interested in moving this company forward with the best focus and intention, so...on that note, I want to address the results with you. Of course, the results were completely confidential, but I did get to read some specific comments and I realize now that there are some concerns, some concerns that run along consistent lines. Some themes, if you will. At this point, I'm just interested in your comments. I'm open to hearing anything additional that you'd like to say."

Everyone shifted a little and looked around at one another. Stephen rapped his fingertips lightly on his chair.

"I feel like I need to tell you all something." Mitch stopped long enough to look at each of them in the eye. "I want you all to know that I am devoted 100% to not only the success of this company...but also to your individual success. I know that our recent track record might have you believing otherwise. That's why your feedback yesterday and today—here and now—is very important to me. I am asking for your honesty today, and please believe me when I say that your comments will not be used against you in any way."

From the corner of his eye, Mitch saw Maxy cock her head, as if he'd said something that reached her for the very first time.

Apparently fired up by being able to speak so freely with Kate less than 24 hours before, Maxy took the lead. "Alright. I'll bite." Leaning forward with her forearms on the table, she addressed her soon to be ex-boss. "You know, since I'm leaving, I wasn't sure about participating in the process. Wasn't sure if anything I'd say would be relevant. But now I know otherwise. I want to ask you, Mitch, what part of your brain do you leave out of your work...and why?"

Stephen raised an eyebrow; now his attention was focused. Alan looked rather confused and uncomfortable and Elizabeth looked a little angry. Even Graham was wide-eyed. Mitch felt the urge to allow the question to shove him back into his chair in a crumpled heap, but he rose to meet it as well as he could instead.

"Well, this seems to be a common theme. This whole idea that I'm leaving something out, not being *authentic*," he said, trying his best not to say what he now referred to as the "a-word" with any sarcasm. At a loss for anything solid to put into words, he continued. "I guess that's what this coaching process is all about. I feel..." In an instant, he realized how uncomfortable he was using the words *I feel*, but continued intentionally. "I feel...like I'm finding answers to questions like that which I didn't know existed. This is not an easy process for me, but I'm going to see it through. You have my word."

The floodgates were open. For the remaining 20 minutes or so of the meeting, Mitch listened to comments about the stagnant environment and the need for more creativity in the workplace, a concept that still seemed so vague to him. Opening up with how much he supported and admired Mitch, Jonathan gently told him that he could no longer rest on his laurels. Mitch was absolutely floored. He'd never considered that his hip, young buddy of a Sales Manager had serious thoughts about much at all...much less that anyone perceived him as resting on *anything*.

Maxy ran with the idea, saying how much *potential* she saw in Mitch and then opening up a dialogue about the competition, about the dynamic, exciting young companies that were popping up with promises of corporate and personal growth potential, the opportunity to travel and to work on an international level with strategic partners. Mitch watched with dismay as eyes around the room lit up.

Graham drove it home. "And we all realize that you assume the team is here for the long haul. But, Mitch, you've got to realize that the 'long haul' has to be motivated from within. No one is mandated to stay. People stay when they love what they do, when they are challenged to take on projects that will stretch them. When they see that love in their leader, it's contagious and inspiring. When they don't, they start to notice it elsewhere."

"If you want us to dig deeper, Mitch, you're gonna have to be the first one to pick up the shovel and get down and dirty," Stephen finally said.

No one had anything to say after that, and the room fell silent. Elizabeth was the first to get up. Graham was the last one out of the room. As he walked toward Mitch, he did a brief, slow-motion, one handed slap-happy-pappy on the outside of his leg, not trying to be funny — just hoping for a spark of realization. When he couldn't catch Mitch's eye directly, he stopped beside his chair. "You know, Mitch, I just don't buy it."

Mitch flashed him a look that said, *Meeting adjourned!* He'd had enough.

Graham continued. Mitch looked down. "When you throw out things like *I am outdamnstanding!,* or any of your other witty comments or comebacks, everybody else concurs. Problem is, it's all corrupted at the source; **you** don't believe it. And as far as Stephen's comment about you 'getting down and dirty,'...do you even remember what that means? I'm sure you once did...but can you stretch yourself that far any more? When the nitty-gritty rears its head, you address it with sarcasm...not substance. When you've had enough of the heat, you vanish from the building. You say that you want our success, individually, collectively. Well, that's what we want for you, too, Mitch. And, you know, you have a wife who wants it for you, too. Frankly, I don't know how she deals with you. Maybe you need to define what you mean by success first...and just how deep you're willing to dig for it. I'll always have your back." With that, he was gone.

Mitch felt winded. He sat back and slumped even further in the chair. When he finally took a breath, it was a deep one, and it frightened him to realize that he'd forgotten to breathe.

"Kate, it was scary as hell," Mitch said just seconds into their next coaching call. "And that's something I wouldn't admit to anybody else...not my team, not anyone. So, I'm honoring you with that info."

Kate acknowledged him. "A lot of leaders would never take that extra step." Mitch had begun rattling off the details about his post-360 meeting with the team. "Right now, I just want you to take a minute and get grounded."

"Thank you," Mitch said after a deep breath.

"On a scale from 1-10, what was the fear like when you were sitting with your team?" she asked.

"I was at an 8. I can imagine that that's what actors or performers describe as stage fright. I was hearing the words, but I felt numb...like I was in a bad dream. I've never felt so vulnerable in my entire life. I had the firing-squad feeling...like they're gonna fire all of this stuff at me, and...I'll be standing there alone," he said.

"Looking back now, on a scale from 1-10, how do you feel?"

"The information itself is great, and I appreciate it. But what was an 8 in fear has gone to probably a 9 or 10 in frustration." Mitch paused for a moment, saying that he felt like he'd gone to Dad for approval, but Dad had just told him everything he'd done wrong and gone to bed, leaving him standing there. "And as far as the team goes, I mean, they like me. Great. They think I'm talented and have lots of *potential*. Great. They think I'm not using all of myself. *Great*. What the hell am I supposed to do with those nuggets?"

Mitch barely heard Kate's next question, caught up in his own rapidly moving train of thought. "You know, I guess what's happened is that, in considering the *truth* from their perspective, I've been forced to look at my own *truth*. And they're right."

"What are they right about?"

"Well, I...I suppose I have been holding back from my team..." Mitch waited for a response from Kate, but she gave him some room. "...in some very personal ways," he finally concluded.

"Mmmhmm," she said, waiting for more.

Mitch finally sat back into the comfort of his leather desk chair, deciding to come clean. "Back when I was a kid, a very young kid, I was a performer." He interrupted himself with a laugh. "And a bit of a director. And my mother, bless her, was the backbone of everything creative I did. I always had her support. Dad, not so much."

Mitch's voice took on a new enthusiasm. "I wrote and directed small plays. You know, with neighborhood kids. And that's an avenue that I always saw laid out before me all the way through high school." He laughed again, going on to explain that stashed in his garage was a box full of every script, play and story he'd ever written, a box that hadn't been opened in twenty years.

"I was the *Will and Grace* writer of my day! Funny stuff. It's what I wanted to do with my life. Come time for college," Mitch continued, punctuating his story with another laugh, "I sent away to UCLA film school for an application, I guess knowing all the while that Dad would never let that happen. Well, when it came in the mail, Dad tossed it at me along with *the look*, something I'd seen only a few times in my life. That was the last time I saw it, and it was the most devastating."

Going on to explain that he'd chosen the University of Virginia and taken a path that, according to Dad, assured him of success, Mitch said he'd told himself that he would never look back.

"I had a girlfriend for a while. A serious one. We talked about marriage..." he inserted a sarcastic laugh. "Ironically, Kate, she...boy, I loved her. She was amazing. She had a passion...and she left for film school. UCLA film school."

With that last laugh, Kate called him out. "You keep laughing, Mitch, as you tell your story. What's that about? What is funny about this?"

He shook his head and chewed the inside of his cheek silently. Tossing his pen on his desk, he finally said that laughing through frustration was a way he'd always coped. "There's something else. Almost no one knows this. When I go out on business trips to big cities, I will usually book an extra day. And that night, I'm sitting in the back of a comedy club—the Laugh Factory, I love it—nursing a cocktail or two. And I become a different person. I dress differently, act differently. It's like I'm flying. I'm so free and light. And I tell no one. So laughter...it goes a long way for me. Always has..."

"I sense that the laughter is more than a humorous diversion for you, Mitch. It's some type of sadness." Kate zeroed in. "Now that I am hearing this, it all makes perfect sense. It's crystal clear that you have left one of the biggest parts of yourself out of your leadership. Your humor, your creativity...you think that you've stashed it safely away in that box in your garage. The thing is, you haven't fooled everyone. It seems that it is peeking through your façade every now and then, just enough to let your savvy team know that there's something there. And they want to see more of it."

The phone line went silent. Mitch got up to pace and look out the window. He pictured himself floating on a raft down the river and out to the ocean.

With another laugh, he finally continued. "Okay. So, I'll write 'em a play...I mean, excuse my sarcasm..."

"And that's another thing. When the creativity subject comes up, I have noticed that you resort to sarcasm," Kate pressed. Checking his watch and seeing that their call was only half over, Mitch lashed out. "You know, frankly, Kate, I think this conversation's going nowhere."

"Mitch, what's going on for you right now?"

"You're just not gonna leave this alone, are you?

"No, I'm not. Have you ever heard the statement 'whatever you resist persists'?" she asked him.

"I was about to make a sarcastic comment, but I guess I won't," Mitch replied.

Kate explained that her experience with coaching had shown her that, often-times, the thing that a person was most defensive about was actually the thing he or she most wanted. Honing her objective, she asked Mitch what he got defensive about in reference to his team.

"Well, my potential," he answered curtly.

"You have so much potential, Mitch," Kate reminded him. She must have deduced that the real issue was *tapping into* his potential, because she started to tie the big picture together. "Let's talk about your frustration with what to do with all of the information from the 360. What can you tap into from this knowledge?"

"Wanna know my knee-jerk reaction to that question? I quit! I quit and go back to UCLA and all the damn things that I wanted to do! ...It's ridiculous..." Mitch rounded out his realistic options with ideas like working in the business end of a production company. "Or I could just flex my creative muscles by dressing up as the cow in the Chick-fil-A ads!"

After a good laugh, they both decided that Mitch was not in the position to decide—then and there—what sort of move he should make, if any.

"It's really not that I dislike my job. It just isn't what I had planned," Mitch explained, half to himself. And he was sincere. Asked specifically what he had planned, he said, "I had planned to go to film school and run a production company."

"So what do you dislike?" she asked.

"I dislike feeling stagnant. I dislike the fact that I'm not using that part of myself that I love. If I'd run a production company, I could've used my strategic thinking skills *and* my love of entertainment. I could have pulled off something big...I could have produced blockbusters. That's what I thought was possible."

"I don't know, Mitch. I'm not convinced. I don't hear your passion."

Mitch was stumped for a moment. "Hmm...I guess maybe I've boxed myself in to one way of thinking. I've relegated my creative talents to just one industry. I never thought of using them outside of that arena." Pressed to consider that idea further, he pulled back. "I feel like I need to come in off the ledge and ponder for a while. This is all new territory. I've never been so honest with anyone before. Ever."

"You know, for someone who is so talented and creative, you seem to spend a lot of time in your head, analytically and critically thinking. Something's telling me that we're at a watershed moment in your life, though. What I see for you is a new opportunity for more creative thinking and brainstorming. It sounds like that's what your team is looking for, too. You might not be ready for it now, but what I see for you is using your creativity more to drive the decisions that you make at home and at work."

After a few moments, all that Mitch could say was a hesitant, "Okay."

"Let me ask you this. When you were that kid writing and producing all that comedy, where did that come from? Did you agonize over *thinking* it into being?" Kate asked.

"No, it... For lack of a better word, it came from my soul. It literally just sort of poured out of me. It was just there."

"What do you do now to get in touch with that part of yourself, Mitch?"

"I don't. I haven't gotten in touch with that part of myself in years."

"That's the fieldwork. Your assignment is to do something to find that part of yourself again. Your team wants it. And I think you want it for yourself," Kate told him. When Mitch asked for more specifics, Kate asked him if structure wouldn't defeat the purpose.

After a deep sigh, he responded. "I guess it would put me back in that comfortable box, wouldn't it?"

"Exactly," Kate responded. "So, my request is for you to pick your own creative outlet over the next week. Let it run wild. Let yourself sit with the idea, the possibilities for the next 24 hours. And not in your head...but in your heart. I want you to close your eyes and visually move the energy from your head and into your chest area...around your heart. My request is that you get very quiet and get back in touch with that creative part of yourself...that part from which things just pour."

Toward that end, Kate took Mitch into a visualization exercise. Asking him to first close his eyes, place his feet on the floor and get grounded, she told him to focus on inhaling and exhaling. "Now, shift your focus from your head to your chest area...feel your heart beating. Now get back in touch with that kid that you were at age 15...age 16. See yourself writing, creating humor and drama. When you're ready, come back and tell me about what you saw."

The line was silent for a minute or so.

"It...hmm...It's a little sad. Frightening. Dad's voice came in...and went away. I'm very visual, cinematic in the way I see most things. Scene one saw me going into the garage and getting down my box. My box full of everything I'd written. And what I saw—this is so corny. I'd never put this in a film! Anyway, what was in the box was my heart...all dusty. Then cut to me at 15. I had written this comedy sketch based on a Laurel and Hardy scene. Brilliant—for a 15-year old. Slapsticky. I borrowed this film camera from a neighbor and made this little 5-minute film. I never felt so alive. There was a smile on my face. I was bringing people together! We were all dynamic and creating this wonderful fun together. It ended with a fade out on Oliver Hardy, looking me square in the eye."

"So, you were able to reconnect with that part of you?"

"I don't know that I trust it, but, yes. There's something there," Mitch replied hesitantly. "There's something there that hinted at—I can't put my finger on it— hinted at the same energy, but with me in a business suit. I have no idea what that means. I think there's something to this, Kate."

"My request is that you revisit the box. I want to ask that somehow you do get back in touch with what that box represents. Coaching's not about living in or rehashing the past, but sometimes we have to get back in touch with it long enough to reignite our passions. That's what I'm asking you to do."

"Alright. I'm willing to play that game."

"How are you feeling?" Kate asked. "We've covered a lot of ground."

"Excited. Scared. You name it."

"Well, just remember that feeling so many emotions and handling them all is a great skill for a leader. So, let yourself just go with the process. And we will reconnect next week. Thank you, Mitch, for your honesty and openness."

Vulnerability

A common fear that all leaders face is the fear of vulnerability. Leaders usually wonder if their peers, team members and employees (and even their family members) will reject them if they reveal their weaknesses. They also question if they will lose their credibility when admitting to mistakes.

In Chapter 11, Mitch makes a very bold move...to discuss the results of his 360 with his team and to get additional feedback. This is a very important step for Mitch because he is willing to be open to the perceptions of his team in order to strengthen his leadership foundation. As a leader, the perceptions of others are your reality. While those perceptions may be skewed and/or unrealistic, they are what people see and believe when they look at you. For Mitchell James, there is one reality...his team is perceiving that he is not leading authentically. How do those whom you lead perceive you?

Coaching Questions:

- How do you feel about being vulnerable to your team?

- What are you afraid will happen if you are vulnerable in front of your team?

- What do you stand to gain by being vulnerable?

- If you allow that part of yourself to be known to your team, what are you concerned will happen?

- If you allow that part of yourself to be known to your team, what do you stand to gain?

THIRTEEN | Truth

"So, are you coming with us, babe?" Anna asked, grabbing some water bottles out of the fridge.

"You know," Mitch replied with a pause, "I think I'm gonna clean out the garage. We'll be headed into spring before you know it, and we'll want to be barbequing and whatnot..." His voice trailed off with a little laugh.

Anna put her hand on her hip, looking at him with a hint of a smirk. "Okay, first...we have an island barbeque, Mitch. It's a permanent fixture on the patio, remember? It's not like you have to haul anything out of the garage to grill some damn burgers. Second, spring won't be in full force for months here. Third, you just used the word *whatnot*. Whatnot? You never say things like that."

Mitch shrugged his shoulders slightly, held his hands palms-up and seemed to be trying to get some kind of reply out of his lips.

"What the *hell* is up with you lately?" Anna asked.

Mitch bit the left inside corner of his bottom lip.

"Are you having an affair or something?"

"Oh, God. Anna, no!" He ran his hand through his already disheveled morning-hair. "No, I am absolutely, definitely, not having an affair. I wouldn't have the energy even if I wanted...Uh, I'm sorry. That was stupid to say. But, no! No, of course not."

"Look, I...I know you're not. I just...At least if you were, I'd know what I was dealing with! I'm not saying I want you to. I just don't understand who you are lately. And if you think the boys don't notice it, too, you'd better think again."

"What are you guys talking about?" a voice said from behind Mitch. He spun around to see Kyle leaning in the doorway with his arms crossed.

"Oh, hon, how long have you...?" Anna walked over to him.

Mitch interrupted her question. "Son, your mom and I are just talking. Everything's fine."

"Can we go?" Kyle asked.

"Yes, yes. I was just getting a few things together," Anna said, giving Mitch the eye. With that, she grabbed the cooler, her purse and her son's arm and headed out the door to another soccer game. Daniel was already waiting in the car.

"Alright! First, CEO of the Year, now Father and Husband of the Year. How many accolades can one man take?" Mitch said aloud to himself as he watched his family drive away through the kitchen window. "And there's the infamous sarcasm. And let's not overlook the fact that I'm talking to myself...again."

He shook his head and made a shot of espresso, glancing at the door that would take him into the garage. Resolving to stick to Plan A, he swallowed the shot in one gulp and headed through the door.

Climbing up the built-in wall ladder to the storage area in the garage, he remembered being a kid and doing the same thing in his parents' garage. He called it his "secret club," the place where he and his friends would steal off to, in younger years to trade baseball cards and eat too many cookies and then, in later years, to look at Playboy magazines...and eat too many cookies.

Shuffling boxes around in the dust, he finally saw it, the old banker's box that he hadn't opened in twenty years or more. "Papers and stuff—Mitch," it said in black ink on the side. Though the dingy, dusty air made him cough, he felt the urge to stay, to just revisit the past in this dark, secluded place.

Finally back in the house, Mitch sat on the couch in the den and stared at the box for a few minutes, as Zoe stared at him from a distance. At last, he lifted the lid, and there they were, all of his old scripts and sketches and films. He traced his finger over the writing, his own, on the top canister. *The Crazy Kid Caper, Go-Cart Alley, The Great Polliwog Hunt!* The urge to swallow hard to keep the nostalgia and grief at bay caught him by surprise. Before he knew it, he was up and hauling Dad's old 8mm projector out of the closet.

"C'mon, Zoe," he said. She knew she wasn't allowed on the couch, so she sat next to his feet on the floor. He followed suit and pulled her so close that she gave him a look of surprise. The two of them settled in to watch some good cinema.

That night, much to his sons' surprise, Mitch came into each of their rooms to tell them goodnight. Sitting there with Kyle, he brushed the boy's hair back and looked into his eyes with absolute wonder, realizing that his son was the same age he'd been when he made his first film.

"Are you okay, Dad?"

"Yeah. Yeah, I'll be fine. I mean, I am. I'm fine. How could I not be with a son like you?" Kyle smiled at his dad but looked a little confused. Mitch continued, "Son, I know that you want to be a soccer player and a pro dirt bike rider and a video game designer...and all of those wonderful things. I, uh," he had to stop to clear his throat. "I want you to know that I'll always be here for you. I'll support you in whatever it is you feel you want to do."

"I know that. You're my dad!"

With that, Mitch wiped his eyes and headed back downstairs to read some old scripts and nurse a martini.

"Well, it was a nice trip down memory lane, Kate, but truthfully, I'm not exactly sure where we're going here," Mitch said during their coaching call later that week. "I was taken on an emotional roller coaster, but, you know, so what? I mean, what are we really accomplishing?"

Mitch finished up an email, trying to be discreet about the tapping of the keys. Before she addressed the question, Kate asked him about memory lane.

"Well, I was the Otto Preminger of my day! A little dictator! I mean, the camera was rolling most of the time, but I was yelling *action!* and *cut!* left and right. Later, when I had the chance to go through the scripts, I also found a couple of full comedy sketches that I never had the chance to perform. A little dated, but funny for 1983. But again, I don't get what this has to do with anything. Sometimes, Kate..." Mitch started to laugh, "Sometimes I think you're a little dizzy."

"Ah, yes....being dizzy keeps me interesting, though, right?"

"Oh, that was meant to be endearing; I hope I didn't offend you."

"Well, Mitch, we've been working together long enough that I can call a spade a spade and say that you are the master of smartassdom. But I can also say that I find it charming, because beneath it all is your brilliant, creative energy. And, now I can see that you stepped into leadership at a young age. You are a natural born leader, Mitch, and you can't tell me otherwise. And besides, I don't offend that easily!"

"I'll try harder…"

They both laughed. "Tell me about this roller coaster ride you experienced."

Mitch tossed the pen he'd been tapping and got up to pace. "Boy, you're like a dog with a bone. Alright, then, I'm just up and down from one day to the next. I don't know how else to describe it."

"What are the specific emotions that you're feeling?"

"It varies from day to day," he said with a sigh. "I think, I think…"

"Wait. I'm gonna stop you right there," Kate said. "I asked you what you're *feeling*, and you're starting to tell me what you're *thinking*. For someone as intelligent as you, I know it's easy to go back into your head, but I'm going to ask you to take a moment and be aware of the emotions themselves."

"Well…sadness, annoyance, frustration, doubt, excitement, wonder—maybe—happiness…yeah…" After a pause he continued. "I feel like I'm missing something."

"What do you feel you're missing?"

Mitch was silent for a moment. He went back to his desk and realized that he'd never put the Orson Wells photo back on the bookshelf. "To answer that, I'm gonna have to go back to me as little Otto Preminger. Maybe I misjudged what I called being a dictator…maybe it was just being passionate. I feel like I've lost that passion. I had it once, clearly. And that is gone. I've realized that over the last few weeks."

"Alright. What about the sadness?"

Mitch explained that he felt like he walked away from the biggest part of him, from the thing he wanted most, the thing he'd assumed he would be. "But it just wasn't acceptable to be what I wanted to be. I had to do other things."

"What did you have to do instead?" Kate pressed.

"I had to make money. I had to be successful. I had to support a family. A mere handful of people in the arts actually make money doing what they love," he answered.

"I'm seeing some black and white thinking here," Kate said. "I think you believe that, in order to use your creative talents, you have to become a starving actor or director. But I also see that the very fact that you're discussing this whole topic openly with me means it's possible that you'll eventually see the entire picture of your life in vivid color...and that you'll bring your creativity—bit by bit—into every aspect of your life. Eventually, that creativity can create the platform on which you will become an authentic leader, Mitch. How does that strike you?"

"A little pie-in-the-sky," he answered curtly. "I mean, I could have taken a crap-shoot at success in the film industry, but I really didn't like the odds that I might still be waiting tables at 50. Not a great way to raise a family. I chose not to make the gamble. But then...maybe I'm not understanding how my type of creativity can fit into my life as it is. So, again, maybe I'm missing something here."

"Alright, I'm going to take a step back here. Mitch, most coaches follow a rigid methodology, a formula if you will, that moves you from A to B to C. I'm a different kind of coach." Kate explained how she relied on client feedback and her own intuition to drive the course of the coaching relationship. She told Mitch that her experience with leaders on an international scope in a variety of industries had shown her that there was no blanket prescription for coaching. The key for her was listening attentively and honing in on not only what the client said, but also what he or she didn't say. "I explain this to tell you that all of these seemingly disparate things we've done—the manifesto, the 360, your revisiting 'the box'—have all been for the purpose of raising your awareness about what you want to hone in on, about this thing that you feel you're missing. They've also been opening your eyes to the possibilities—whatever they may be."

Mitch listened, and Kate continued. "Most coaches would have asked you this question right out of the gate, and while we touched on it in our initial conversation, I've intentionally delayed it to allow you to gain some perspective. So, I ask you now, what do you really want to achieve as a result of working with a coach?"

"Well, the answer is clear. The Board wants the numbers up and the talent to stick around," Mitch answered curtly, noticing that only twenty minutes of their hour-long appointment had passed.

"That's what the Board wants. What I want to know today is what *you* hope to gain from this coaching process," Kate said without mincing words.

"You mean what would be a nice perk, a nice by-product of me bringing up the numbers and retaining talent?"

"Well, that could be part of it. But you're skirting your own issues, Mitch. Let me put this in familiar terms. You're writing a role for yourself as a leading man and then throwing away the script before it's done. What do you want for your life?"

Mitch was silent. "Alright," he finally said with a deep sigh. "Let me preface this by saying that it's what I want but don't know how to get. I want…"

"Wait," Kate interrupted. "Don't go to the how yet. I just want you to answer the question. You're writing a role for yourself as a leading man and then throwing away the script before it's done. What do you want for your life?"

"I guess I always get mired in the how-to of the logistics instead of just letting myself dream."

"So, without going into the how…let's stay on what you want. What do you really want, Mitch?"

"I want...I want that passion that I had as a 12-year old. That kid-behind-the-camera feeling. I want it in my work...with my kids...I *really* want it with Anna. With everything...I don't even know what I'm saying..."

Kate called his attention to how soft and quiet his voice had become. "Well, sure, Kate. I just admitted that I'm leading, in some ways, a passionless existence," he said, barley audible. "It's hard."

When she asked him how willing he was to explore the subject, he said the whole thing was a bit touchy-feely for him but that he was curious.

"What is touchy-feely?"

"Well, I'm curious about the method to your madness, where we're going."

"Hmm. I think what you're really getting curious about is how you're going to get your passion back," Kate said, point blank.

Mitch let go his characteristic on-the-spot-chuckle. "Ah, always cuts to the chase. Okay, yes. I want to know how you suppose I'm going to get my passion back. Curious to the point of incredulous, but I'll set that aside."

"Okay. I feel like we can make some progress now because I sense that you are starting to engage yourself in the process and feel part of your own coaching rather than standing outside, looking for the methodology of it," Kate said before proceeding.

To address Mitch's question about the connection between his creativity and the profits and talent, she took him back to a conversation they'd had about the 360-assessment. "So you're saying that you want to feel passionate again and talking about all of these parts of yourself that you've kept secret. How does this conversation that we're having today relate to your team wanting you to be a more authentic leader?"

"Well, they said that I leave a part of myself out of my work. And if I think of that comment in terms of my life...I suppose I'm not authentic. I've never told anyone the things I've told you. Sure, Anna knows vaguely that I used to sort of have an interest in film, but no one knows that I spend an extra day on business trips to immerse myself in comedy clubs and become another person!"

"What are you afraid would happen if people knew the truth?" Kate asked.

Mitch hemmed and hawed, talking about painful memories and not wanting to burden others. He finally just concluded by saying, "It's irrelevant. I need to get a job done."

"Something tells me that you're afraid your team and employees won't take you seriously if they know about your creative talents and passions and your humor."

"Well, come on. If I'm standing at the water cooler doing my Groucho Marx impression, who the hell's gonna consider me credible when I'm leading a meeting?" Mitch asked rhetorically.

"Come on Mitch. I don't buy that! Sounds like an excuse to me," Kate said. She told Mitch he was smart enough to know when to play which cards where and with whom. She reiterated the team's confidentiality with their feedback, saying that all she did was ask a series of questions; it was the team that came forth with wanting more authenticity from their leader. "They're sharp, Mitch. They see mere winks of your creativity but feel deprived by not being let in on what they seem to intuitively know is your big secret. They feel that your secret could make you a better leader. Does that make sense?"

"Well...sure, I guess. But why didn't someone just save all the hassle and tell me what everyone was saying?"

Kate asked him to answer that question for himself. When he guessed that people were perhaps afraid that he'd be angry, and Kate questioned him, he finally admitted that he'd never lost his cool with anyone at work. "My impression,

Mitch, is that your team didn't tell you not because they dislike you and enjoy talking behind your back, but rather because they adore you. They want to protect you from any painful truth they can."

"I'm no china doll. I don't want people to protect me," Mitch said, taken aback.

"Mitch, if you understood the twinkle in your own eyes that draws people to you, makes them want to listen to you, inspires them to look for your directives, you'd also understand why they are protective of you. They feel a definite loyalty to you. I know I only spent a short time at your office, but I can walk into a room and feel whether the team fears or adores their leader. Your team would go to the moon for you, Mitch."

"Yeah, well, Maxy would not be on that expedition."

"Oh, yes, so what about Maxy?" Kate asked.

"Gone. She's gone. Not so loyal."

"What about her leaving makes you say that she's not loyal?"

Mitch quoted all of what he considered Maxy's touchy-feely, growth oriented goals, ending with "blah, blah, blah..."

Kate pressed on. "On a scale of 1-10, Mitch, how loyal were you to Maxy and what she requested?"

"How **loyal**?! What do you mean...? I gave her incredible opportunities!"

"On a scale of 1-10, with 10 being the highest, how much did you meet Maxy's touchy-feely, growth oriented goals?" Kate persisted.

Mitch let go an exasperated sigh. "I don't know how to answer that question."

The line was silent. "Are you there?" Silence. "There you are. You're doing that silent thing you do. Okay, okay. I get it. I can play this game. Testing, testing, one, two..." Mitch tapped the phone as if it were a microphone and then burst into the rhythm of a vaudevillian show tune.

"Okay, are you done with the show?"

"What do you mean by that?" Mitch asked, offended.

"What I mean is that when I get silent, you default to sarcasm and your song and dance routines. You do it when things get tough. And *I don't know how to answer that question* has become a pat reply for you. So, what's the song and dance routine about?"

"What's the silence about? Answer me that."

"You are good at getting off topic. The silence is about giving you room to sit with, consider and address the tough questions, Mitch. Also, honestly, I just feel sometimes like I need to be silent. I don't ask you questions to try to sound smart or intuitive. I ask you questions that are truly relevant. So, I ask you again. What's the song and dance routine about?"

"...while I whistle a happy tune!" Mitch quipped, quoting a line from *The King and I*.

"Mitch, cut it out!"

"Comedy, Kate. Isn't that how the song goes, my all-knowing coach? 'Make 'em laugh, make 'em laugh, make 'em laugh...' Entertaining people is a diversionary tactic, one that I learned to use at a very young age. Get 'em laughing, put up the smoke screen, and they won't notice that your feet aren't on the beat."

Mitch gave another sigh of exasperation, telling Kate how uncomfortable she made him sometimes. Still, she pressed on, asking how her letting him off the hook would help him bring up numbers, retain talent, and become an authentic leader.

"At least I could have a professional conversation that didn't hinge on my deep, dark secrets and cliffhanger questions," he said.

"I'm not buying it. I think you are loving these tough questions. I think that there's a part of you that loves relinquishing control a bit and that relishes reviving the part of you that you left behind. Mitch, you are a top player, and I don't let top players off the hook."

The line was silent except for a brief, "Hmm" from Mitch.

"We've talked about Tiger Woods. Do you think that his coach lets him off the hook? Better yet, do you think that Tiger lets himself off the hook?" Kate asked.

After a smartass reply about his coach doing whatever Tiger and all his money told him to do, he said, "My honest reply would be that you don't achieve that level of talent by getting off the hook."

"Thank you for illustrating my point so nicely. Mitch, I consider you to be at the Tiger Woods level of talent in the world of international trade. So, I'm not backing off. That being said, I will tell you that I see some repeating patterns in your game. There's a connection between your lack of passion, your lack of authenticity, the diversionary song and dance routines and your lack of creativity in the workplace. Your team sees it all. You've been asking from day one what your personal life and your creativity have to do with your professional life. I've been thinking that the only person who doesn't see the connection...is you. But you know what? I am now getting the feeling that somewhere deep inside, you know exactly how this all matches up. Am I correct or way off base?"

Mitch felt a stirring in his gut, a sensation that had become increasingly familiar over the last several weeks, and flashed back to the question that Maxy had shot at him after the 360. *Mitch, what part of your brain do you leave out of your work...and why?*

Truth

What does it really mean to *lead from a place of truth?*

When I ask this question of leaders, I usually hear something like "Well...it means to be honest" or "It means to live with integrity." But I believe that leading from a place of truth goes much deeper. Leading from a place of truth means leading according to who you really are and honoring **and using** the many gifts and talents with which you were blessed at birth and never ever forgetting your roots and your life story. Your family, your culture and your unique experiences...simply because they are yours, they are meaningful.

As a coach, I do not work with leaders on healing their past, but I do encourage them to revisit significant past events and to tell stories about those times to inspire their followers and to get in touch with their truth.

Coaching Questions:
As you move toward your own truth, ask yourself these questions:

- What part of your life, your brain or your past are you leaving out of your life as a leader?

- If you reveal this part of yourself to your followers, what are you concerned will happen?

- What are your roots? Where were you born, who is your family, and what culture shaped who you are today?

- How often do you talk about your roots to your followers? If not at all, why not?

- How can you use the stories of your youth and your life experiences in a way that will inspire your followers?

- Where in your life are you apologizing for being who you are? And why?

FOURTEEN | Authenticity

"So what's up? You've hardly shown your face outside of your office for almost two weeks now~are you cheating on me with another friend?" Graham joked, not missing a beat as he took another bite of his tuna melt.

"You sound like my wife..." Mitch said before he had time to edit himself.

"What?"

"Nothing..." Mitch answered, but the comment was not lost on Graham. Mitch dove in to his coleslaw. "Hey, I thought we said we were gonna quit this deli. The warm cheese smell and shitty coffee?"

"It seems to be our default. Speaking of default settings, how goes the coaching? I mean, old patterns are tough to break," Graham said.

Mitch set his sandwich back on the plate, quite intentionally. "The coaching. The coaching is...is fine. You know, to be honest, I've thought a lot about what you and Stephen said to me that day during our 360 meeting–though I hate to admit that I've paid attention to anything Stephen says. You know, the whole idea about being able to get 'down and dirty,' to roll up my sleeves and dive into...to my life and my work. Well, that's kind of what Kate and I have been working on, too."

"Really? Just *kind of?*"

"I can't get a break! Neither one of you misses a thing. Okay, it's what we've been working on *whole-heartedly*. This whole *authenticity* idea. It's the new A-word for me, you know. But…" Mitch said, resuming his sandwich and talking with his mouth full, "I'm trying to set aside my incredulity and just proceed."

"Well, that's great news! The bad news is that your table manners really suck. I'm appalled at times."

"You should be used to it by now," Mitch teased. "My latest 'assignment' was to read some articles on authentic leadership. And I did it!" Mitch said with mock aplomb, sitting up straight and dotting the corners of his mouth with his napkin.

"That's more like it…on both counts…the homework completion and the etiquette," Graham said. "Hold that thought…" he added, getting up to refill his coffee.

Great, Mitch thought. "So what's your question?" he asked when Graham sat back down again. "Come on, I recognized the dramatic pause in the conversation. Go ahead, dive in."

"I'm impressed. Alright, then, first I have to say that I'd love to read those articles," Graham said.

"Of course you would. They're right up your alley. You can add 'em to your touchy-feely catalogue of human growth and spiritual development resources. Or we can discuss 'em round the campfire."

"Nah," Graham said. "That would necessitate wearing cruddy jeans. I don't do cruddy jeans. But in the meantime, spill it."

Mitch stopped mid-chew. "What?"

"Tell me about that Orson Welles picture you've had in your office since day one. You know, the one that conveniently disappeared before Miss Kate made her appearance," Graham said.

Mitch finished chewing slowly, sat back in his chair and cracked his knuckles. Graham winced at the sound.

"Alright. Okay. My team wants me to be *authentic*, to own up to my creative side. I'll start with you, give you the details that the rest of the team doesn't need. Do you know what I have in my garage?"

"A whole lot of shit you don't need. And a box of vintage Playboys that just might come in handy—so to speak—if your wife gets tired of the same old song and dance."

Mitch smiled and shook his head. "Touché. I should know better than to ask you rhetorical questions. Let me tell you a little story." Mitch tossed his napkin on top of what was left of his sandwich. "I used to know this kid. He was lanky and tallish. He did okay in school, but he was really too busy reading film scripts and books on cinema to care much about geometry. He loved to spend summers with his grandparents because he and Grandpa would spend countless hours watching Beta and then VHS copies of old comedic acts...Buster Keaton, Laurel and Hardy, the Marx Brothers.

"When the boy was 11, he and Grandpa watched *Citizen Kane* together. That got him started on classic dramas, Orson Welles films in particular. The boy told Grandpa that he wanted to write great stories and make films like that, ones that would make people laugh and cry. Grandpa told him that he could do whatever he put his mind to and that he'd always be there for him. Well, the boy's dad had other ideas. And Grandpa knew it.

"The boy spent summer days while Dad was at work making 8mm movies with the neighborhood kids. Mom was on the boy's side and she let him use Dad's camera on the sly. She was cool, that mom. Grandpa loved to watch the movies with the boy. He even stored them at his house 'til the boy was grown.

"Grandpa was also a collector of valuable antiques. When the boy turned 15, Grandpa gave him an autographed picture of Orson Welles that he'd been saving for him. The boy resolved to go to film school. When it came time, Dad intercepted the college application from the mail, tossing it at the boy and making it very clear that no son of his would make a mockery of all of his hard work.

"The boy acquiesced. Then, in college, he fell in love with a girl named Rory. It was one of those idealistic loves, based on passionately shared interests. The girl never knew how much the boy loved her, how much she inspired him. When it came time for grad school, the girl left. She headed out west. UCLA film school. Irony at its finest. Another irony...Maxy looks a lot like the girl did...and has that same..." Mitch paused for a deep breath. "...that same undeniable passion for her work, for everything. The boy used to have that passion."

Suddenly self-conscious, Mitch looked around the deli, hoping that no one had overheard him. Graham was quiet. He cleared his throat.

"Don't do the silence thing. Kate does that. I don't have anything more to say right now," Mitch said.

"I think the boy still has it, that passion. I know you laugh at my being such a linguaphile, but I've got a definition for you. Authenticity is partially defined as something like, 'of undisputed origin.' Mitch, you'll never make mutually exclusive who you were and who you are. And as long as you keep trying, no one's gonna buy your act. How much of this story does Anna know?"

Mitch shifted in his seat. "Very little."

"About your work with Kate?"

"Even less. I've told her that I'm 'addressing some issues with a mentor.'"

Graham leaned his elbows on the table. "I say this with utmost respect for you, my friend. You need to take a closer look at the meaning of authenticity."

"Well, at least you didn't call me Grasshopper," Mitch quipped.

"I hate to say it, but I was actually thinking more along the lines of *coward*."

Authenticity

Pick up just about any book or article on the topic of leadership and you will almost always find a list of qualities and characteristics that the author feels makes for a great leader. Most of these lists lack one quality: authenticity. I believe that authenticity is essential for leaders of today and tomorrow. Finding and stepping into your authentic self is not an easy task. Leaders are pulled in multiple directions each day by team members, board members, clients, family members, friends and strategic partners, and each person comes to the leader with their own set of expectations. By becoming an authentic leader, you will find that you no longer feel the need to play multiple roles or to emulate someone else's leadership style. With authentic leadership, you live according to who you are...the values and the purpose of your life as defined by **you**.

In Chapter 14, Mitch takes his first stab at trying on his authenticity by sharing a part of his life with Graham. He feels sure that he will be safe with Graham and knows that opening up to another human being about the whole of his life is a critical first step in getting comfortable in his authentic skin.

Coaching Questions:

- What is your purpose in life?

- How is your purpose in life important to your ability to build an authentic leadership style?

- In what areas of your leadership are you trying to lead like someone else? How does that style work both for you and against you?

- If you could lead exactly according to who you are, how would you lead? Be as descriptive as possible.

- Think of a situation in your business or personal life where you are compromising your authenticity simply to make people happy. If you fail to make everyone happy, what do you think will happen to you?

- When was the last time you really fought for something you believe in? Why did it feel so important to fight for this cause? (What values and philosophies were at play?)

- What are your greatest assets? Do you bring each of these assets into your leadership style? If not, why not?

- How can your strengths also be viewed as a weakness by your followers? (Example: If being a compassionate listener is one of your strengths, your followers may see that you spend too much time listening and not enough time taking action.) What steps can you take to find some middle ground so that your assets work **for** both you and your team rather than against you?

FIFTEEN | Blindsided

"Morning, Mitchell," Stephen said, catching him by surprise. Mitch quickly scooped up his old tattered, decorated Pee Chee folder from the counter—it had been another one of the things stored in the box in the garage, another casualty of his latent creativity, a symbol of his identity in the early college years.

"Damn, I was gonna say don't worry, I won't spill my coffee on your report, but it looks more like you mugged a high school kid on the way in today. Boss, we've got lined paper in the supply closet, remember? We *can* still afford it; our numbers aren't *that* bad," Stephen joked.

*Of all the people...*Mitch thought, fumbling. "College kid, actually," he said, taking his coffee to leave and regretting that he'd not taken home his briefcase the night before to stash the folder in this morning. The classic "Pee Chee" folder was practically an enduring icon of public schools and community colleges. Like his peers, he'd covered his with band references and logos and clever pop culture phrases. He'd even done the classic makeover on it—with their Bic pens, high school and college kids everywhere transformed the logo that said "Pee Chee All Season Portfolio" to "*Kissing is* Pee Chee, *but sex is an* All Season Sport." Mitch wished he'd been a little more discreet and couldn't wait to stuff the tattered thing in a manila envelope.

Halfway down the hall to his office, he questioned something. Stephen's manner had been as abrasive as always, but had his tone seemed a little less biting since the 360 meeting? *Nah,* Mitch reasoned. *I was just caught off guard.*

In the comfort of his office, Mitch relaxed into his chair and stretched before inhaling a big gulp from his mug. Thoughts that he was both doing the right thing and that he was about to make an idiot of himself wrestled for top billing in his mind.

Opening the old folder, he saw two things that he hadn't seen in years, his ever unsent film school application and his *Citizen Kane* script. With an unexpected surge of old memories, Mitch suddenly remembered how the script had gotten its coffee stain on the top right corner. He and Rory had taken a spring break trip to Toronto. The first day there, they'd gone into a shop that sold vintage books, movie posters, memorabilia and scripts. He'd found *Citizen Kane* immediately and bought it, telling Rory that it was a tribute to his grandfather. Later that afternoon, she'd spilled her coffee on it. To Mitch's surprise, he'd found her so endearing—how she clamored to clean it up and save the script.

They'd stayed at the cheapest hotel they could find, eaten bagels in the mornings, taken in the city by daylight, enjoyed lunch time sex breaks and, after dinner, some nightlife and some beer or wine before heading back to the room to be naked and warm again.

Running his hand over the cover page, he struggled with a vague feeling of lament. Even if he had time to think about having that much sex, he certainly couldn't pull it off anymore. At the same time, he felt a sense of wonder at how the suite hotels with Jacuzzi tubs didn't equate to better sex than hotels with sun-bleached curtains and leaky faucets. Just then, he noticed writing on the inside pocket of the folder. *Perception is everything.* It was Rory's handwriting. Still there. Twenty some odd years later.

"Mr. James, Alan is here to see you," the voice on the intercom interrupted him. He'd temporarily forgotten about the early morning meeting.

"Right, yes. Send him in," Mitch said, closing the folder and setting it behind him on the bottom shelf of the metal cart that held his pressing to-do items.

"Alan, good morning. A pleasure to see you."

Alan pushed up his glasses. "You too, Mr. James," he said, taking a seat.

"To what do I owe the pleasure? What's on your mind?"

"Well, I...I wanted to...First of all, I want to wish you good luck with working with Ms. Nelson. She seems great," he continued with an awkward and completely transparent smile. "I also want to let you know that I will be leaving for another position."

Mitch couldn't believe what he heard and resisted the urge to say *What?! You?!* His second thought was that he'd underestimated his seemingly passive CIO. After several moments of incredulous silence, Mitch finally spoke up. Resisting the urge to belt out *You couldn't have chosen a worse time!* he said, "Alan, I wish you would reconsider. We're poised to be..." Mitch stopped short, realizing that he'd overused that phrase to the point that it sounded like watered-down rhetoric, even to himself. "I value your contributions more than I've been able to express in the past. You are razor sharp with everything you do. Your technology and information skills are so suited for this company, and your understanding of how it all fits into the world of international trade is not something easily understood. What can we offer you to stay? An increase in pay? More time off? Flex hours? I'll talk to the Board; you name it."

Alan pushed up his glasses again, looking more frustrated than interested.

Then Mitch heard himself utter a word that hadn't slipped through his lips since he couldn't remember when. "Alan, *please...*"

"No, no, I just can't, Mr. James. There's...there's just too much going on here.

I'm leaving for a great opportunity, but I do appreciate the experience here. And I thank you," he concluded with a slight nod of his head.

"Well, Alan, I wish you all the luck in the world. Of course, Leslie will conduct an exit interview with you, and I'll need to speak at greater length with you, too, next week to discuss how to best proceed and to handle your projects." Mitch paused, trying to swallow the lump in his stomach. "I'm...I'm sorry that we weren't able to meet your needs. And that I...I wasn't more available to you."

Alan nodded, smiled a more genuine smile than he had earlier and then left just as quickly as he'd come in. Mitch took off his glasses and noticed that his hand was shaking as he ran it through his hair. Resisting the urge to curl into a fetal position in his chair, he put his head down on the desk and drew his knees up slightly for but a moment. The lump in his stomach had become an ache, and he swallowed the bitter taste of coffee and stomach acid that lurched into his mouth. He remembered creating his own opportunities to stand in the spotlight on his climb to CEO...times when the big grin came naturally and he couldn't wait to speak his mind. Now, sitting crumpled in his chair, he couldn't even imagine looking anyone in the eye, much less actually having something worthwhile to say, least of all to the Board.

Blindsided

Leaders occasionally get "blindsided" by something that catches them off guard and seems to magically appear overnight. In reality, these jarring disruptions usually evolve subtly over a number of months or years and often result directly or indirectly from the CEOs lack of sharp decision making.

Coaching Questions:

- Think of a time in the past when you felt blindsided. What subtle signs actually evolved over time, trying to tell you that something negative threatened to happen down the road?

- How did your decision making or lack of it over time contribute to getting blindsided?

- What was getting in the way of your ability to truly "see the writing on the wall?" (Overwhelm, being overly trusting, ignoring your intuition?)

- When have you noticed yourself ignoring your intuition telling you that some type of negative consequence was just around the corner? What can you do, starting today, to pay close attention to your intuitive hits/gut reactions?

BONUS: In order to support you in answering these and other questions pertaining to the subject of being **Blindsided**, Carol Dickson Carr, President of Managing Personal Resources, has provided readers of *Edge* with a **Facing Challenges** audio and action guide. To gain access to this guide, please visit http://www.Edge-book.com/bonus.

SIXTEEN | Doubt

With the articles on authentic leadership that Kate had emailed him two weeks before sitting in front of him on the desk, Mitch leafed through them again. He'd surprised himself by not just giving them a cursory once-over on the computer screen, but actually printing them out and even highlighting them here and there. He'd read them the other day before he decided to bring in the script and UCLA application to show to Graham. And he'd read them again this morning. Just over 30 pages altogether.

Sitting there now before picking up the phone, he remembered telling Kate (rather pompously, he had to admit in retrospect) during their first or second phone call that he didn't get *bogged down in minutiae.* Now it occurred to him that maybe—just maybe—some of the things he'd once considered *minutiae* would actually not *bog* him at all; in fact, they might free him. He tried to dismiss that thought as quickly as possible, but there was something kind of appealing about it.

Mitch told Kate that while the word *authenticity* still kind of made him want to hurl, one article* in particular hit home with him. One of the profiles focused on a man named "Josh," an executive in one of the world's largest television production companies and an early innovator of the documentary genre.

"The thing that struck me was that, with his climb up the corporate ladder, he'd lost his edge and become austere and distant...and he was losing team members left and right. Let me read a piece of this; it says, 'so we coached Josh to return to the mischievous sense of humor that he had displayed more readily earlier in his career. He has an amazing sense of comic timing, which he has learned to use to devastating effect to disarm opponents and delight his followers.' Kind of hit home for me...that letting that part of his personality shine would draw people to him...and keep them there. I don't think that I'm austere, but I can definitely relate to the rest of it."

"What comes to mind when you think of being austere?" Kate asked.

"Cold, controlling, unapproachable. I think that my team sees me at almost the opposite end of the spectrum. One of things that really struck me in the 360 feedback was when you said that you think they feel the need to protect me. As if I'm weak and need to be taken care of. So, frankly, if people *like* me to the point of feeling the desire or need to protect me...then I'd rather be austere," Mitch answered.

"So, do you think that your team considers you to be a weak leader?"

Mitch paused. "No one used the word *weak,* and I don't think that anyone would think in that exact term."

"But you used the word weak," Kate said.

"Yes, I suppose I did. Let me see if I can rephrase this. I know my team thinks I'm smart. But if they think that I need to be taken care of and tiptoed around... then I guess *I'm* actually starting to wonder if I'm a weak leader."

"I'm seeing some black and white thinking here again. I'm sensing that you feel you must either be weak or be austere. And it seems like you're assuming that your team is using broad brush strokes in their opinions of you," Kate said.

"Well, isn't that true?"

"I don't know. While the 360 suggests that there are some leadership issues to address, my observations tell me that your team is clearly still following you," Kate answered.

Mitch sighed. "Well, some of them are following me. But, let's face it, one of the things that's thrown me for a loop is the fact that Maxy and...well, now Alan... Did I tell you about Alan?" Mitch explained that Alan was leaving, too, and that, while it was hard to get much information out of him on any subject, he felt it was probably for a lot of the same reasons that Maxy was leaving and that Maxy might even have brought him along with her to the competition. "Sure, some people are following me, and some people are going AWOL. And that sucks."

"What do you think is causing people to go AWOL?" Kate said.

"I don't always know. I don't think that Leslie ever really gives me the full story, but I do know that Maxy told me point blank following the 360 that I was not giving her opportunities that challenge her."

"Mitch, what do you think your team really wants from you?" Kate asked.

Mitch chuckled. "If I could answer that question, we probably wouldn't be having this conversation."

Kate did the silent thing again, and this time Mitch didn't resort to sarcasm.

"Okay. Here goes. Like I said, part of me still wants to roll my eyes every time I hear the word *authenticity,* and part of me is...really kind of excited about this whole idea." Mitch held the phone between his ear and shoulder and cracked his knuckles one by one. He explained how he'd been rehashing significant interactions he'd had over the last six months that hadn't gone as planned and playing out in his mind how they might have gone differently with some creative thinking ...with a little more of his unique, authentic style in the mix.

"My mind started to spin off...and I let it go," Mitch continued, his tone lifting slightly. "I was mediating this work conflict a while back. I realized that it didn't go as well as it could have because I didn't allow myself to step back and disarm. I actually felt myself becoming more aggressive. In fact, though my intentions were good, things actually escalated because I came to the situation with...with my ego and expectations, I guess."

Mitch got up to pace, talking with his hands as if he had an actual audience. "And I just continued this mental riff! I thought about how I handle conflict with my kids...how I step back and take a lighter tone. I'm just more open. And..." Standing in front of the window now, a slight smile came over his face. "...This whole new way of thinking sort of descended on me. I mean, I was like a crazy person. I'm driving to work in my car, having an out-loud conversation, going over and over different things I could have said, different tones, different inflections. It was kind of energizing..."

"Hmm..." Kate said, giving him room to continue the roll he was on.

"From there, I thought about what I told you about likening myself to a little Otto Preminger as a kid, directing my films. Again, my mind was just going..." He explained to Kate how, while directors have an absolute vision of how everything will look and sound—from the play or film as a whole, to individual scenes, to the shortest of lines—they walk a fine line between staying true to their vision and respecting the actors' interpretation. "To be a successful director, you have to learn how to speak the language of the people you work with. You then go in, meet them where they are and work with them to bring out their best performance. You enlist them in your vision by being enthusiastic about their unique gifts. The analogy or metaphor in that for me as a leader is incredibly powerful! The skills are identical!" Mitch was quiet for a moment. "I have to tell you, Kate, it's a little overwhelming."

"Wow!" Kate said. "Before we go into overwhelm, I have to say that I haven't seen you this passionate or excited in the whole time we've been working together. You are making the connections between who you were as a child director and who you are today as a leader. That's powerful."

Mitch sighed. "I hope you're right. Intellectually, yes, I get it."

"I hear some doubt. What's that about?" Kate asked.

The line was silent.

"The first article in that series you sent me..." Mitch finally said. "The title was *Why Would Anybody Be Led By You?* That right there...that question...that's where I live...every day. Sure, I know I'm smart. I know I am one of the best when it comes to international trade. I know I did a damn good job directing as a kid. People listened to me. I had things to say back then. But...nothing was riding on any of that. It was what it was. In my life today...as CEO in this business, there's a lot riding on my back. Every day on my way to work, I truly doubt that I can lead this company."

"So, Mitch, let me ask you point blank, why would anyone be led by you?"

"I have no idea. No idea." Mitch waited for a response that didn't come. "The silent thing again..." he said with a chuckle.

Kate spoke first. "I will say this. I have observed something in life. The greatest leaders of the world have never said, *Oh, I'm authentic...I'm a great leader.* Their followers are the ones who reach those opinions, and if they feel you are a great leader, they will follow you. Those who are led answer that question...not those who lead. Many great leaders don't even realize the depth and scope of their influence. Read any biography or autobiography of a great leader, and you'll read about doubt at almost any given step. But there's a fine line between humility and lack of self-confidence. What I'm hearing from you is the latter."

"Well, yeah..." Mitch said with a hint of the old sarcastic laugh returning.

"What is creating the lack of self confidence?"

"Maxy and Alan leaving! And let me tell you, all of these articles, everything we've discussed...all well and good. Lovely. Brilliant. But...it feels like it's calling for a complete and total overhaul. Everything I do, everything I say, every part of this organization...I'm going to have to examine and change. Because *perception is everything*...and it's easier to establish a perception than it is to change it." He went on to say how, sure, his success had been laced with struggles, but he'd never hit a wall before. Now—thanks to the 360—before him stood a wall of information that seemed insurmountable.

"Mitch, take a deep breath. Next, remember that this journey to leading authentically is a **process**. It's not something that you can tackle with a laundry list that you check off task by task. You've made some first steps into your authentic leadership style. You have taken the bold step of listening to your team tell you what they want to see in you. Your team wants to see that creative side—the part of you that they say they see missing—in the work place. Again, I believe that there's a connection there between your team wanting that from you and you being able to attract and retain great talent. That connection will gain strength as you rebuild rapport and trust with your team."

Mitch gave a vague affirmative response and rested his elbow on the arm of his chair, running his hand through his hair. He noticed the time and took off his glasses.

"Mitch, we have about 15 minutes left, and I want to talk with you about an assignment I want you to take on for the week," Kate said.

Mitch sat up straight, relieved at shifting the focus...for a few seconds.

"This activity is going to give you a different look at authenticity..."

Ah, the a-word again. So much for that! he thought, resting his elbows on the desk.

"It's an environment assessment tool I use with leaders to help them start looking at things in the environment," Kate continued. "It'll help you see where you're lined up and where you're not."

Mitch had no idea what she was talking about. Kate explained that, in this arena, she pulled from the research and methodology of one of the founders of the profession of coaching, Thomas Leonard, who held that every element of a person's daily life is considered to be an environment. "The books you read, the colors in your office, the people you spend time with, the food you eat, the thoughts you think...they're all environments. Each of your environments expresses who you are and affects your outcomes. It's important that you and your environments accurately reflect one another. For instance, if you hate purple and your office is painted purple...why? If you're talking with people who drain you... why? It's about taking a look at the decisions you make and the ways they play out in the environment around you."

Kate went on to explain that she'd be sending him a 50-point checklist, asking him to use it as a simple guide to help him start asking questions and raise his own awareness around what in his environment felt authentic and what was creating any type of dissonance. "More important than using any kind of objective list is your making notes. You know, use a legal pad or a notebook...something to collect your thoughts and observations."

"Okay, so anything from why I have that damned ficus tree in the office to why I indulge my wife's horrible uncle with small talk, eh!?"

"Ah, yes...I always get the family questions," Kate said, laughing. "What we can do there is work to shift your own responses, help you find some humor in all of the quirks and irritations. And, of course, that perspective works in the office, too. There are always people and situations you'd rather avoid. The trick is, again, to just let people know who you are while not indulging in full disclosure."

"Well, speaking of disclosure," Mitch said, not missing the opening, "You've been here to the offices. What do you think of our environment?"

Kate sighed. "Well, first a disclaimer. I do have some personal biases, so just bear that in mind. My father was an architect and my mother an amazing musician; I have an innate, artistic design sense. So, I don't want to sway you with specific suggestions, but I can offer my general perceptions. When I first entered the building, I felt like it was very open, modern, high tech, forward moving. I was impressed. I got the feeling that this organization was buzzing with excitement... that something big was going on here. Then, though, as I got back into the actual office space—where you work and live most of the day—I felt like I'd gone through a time warp. It felt stark, lacking in creativity, clustered with cubicles. Very late 70's, early 80's. To be honest, Mitch, I felt like the environment was stuck in the past. Does that make sense?"

"It's the disco ball, isn't it? See, I've been saying it should go, but the Board is rather attached to it..." Mitch joked, and they both laughed. From there, he got frustrated, saying that he had no control over wrangling money to revamp the entire building. "So I don't know what to do about that! Sometimes you have to go with what you have."

"On a scale of 1-10, how happy do you feel your team—who is desiring more creative energy in the workplace—is with cubicles?" Kate pressed.

"Well...about a 2 or 3. I'll be the first to say that they don't exactly inspire creativity, but like I said..." His voice trailed off for a second. "So, what, Kate? Now—on top of everything else—I'm supposed to go to the Board with a song and dance about redesigning the freakin' building!?"

"You know...you're right. I apologize as your coach for getting too deeply into the design topic," Kate said, taking a step back. "Seeing you inspired got me inspired and I went with it, but let's just go with the initial environment assessment for now. I know that you've got a lot on your mind to deal with."

Mitch was relieved, and Kate steered the conversation back to its roots. "What in your life, Mitch, do you most value?"

"Family...definitely my family. Loyalty. Hard work. Intellect. I value, um... responsibility. Integrity. Should I go on?"

"What about the creativity that you were fired up about earlier?"

"Well...I used to value that..." he answered.

"You *used* to value creativity? Where did it go?" Kate asked.

"It didn't have a part in what I was creating," Mitch answered softly.

"Look, the values you listed are awesome; don't get me wrong. But you're leaving out a few that I have noticed in you...in the excitement in your voice when you talk about them."

Mitch struggled with the silence for what seemed like a long time. "Wow...it's gonna be quite a week. You're asking me to restructure 20-plus years of basically the same way of thinking...to start from scratch."

"I beg to differ on that idea. Your creativity, your humor...everything you were isn't gone. It's a part of who you are; it's still in you; there's no starting from scratch! You're halfway there. You've exhumed that authentic part of yourself from that box in your garage. You've dusted it off. I see that now you're fighting with the urge to place it on a shelf. Well, your environment—and the environment that your team is looking for—seems to want to support you in letting it leap down from there and play. And remember...the environment is a direct reflection of you, Mitch...like it or not. And I think that, if you let yourself come out to play, you'll like it, too."

*Goffee, R. and Jones, G. "Managing Authenticity: The Paradox of Great Leadership. To attract followers, a leader must be many things to many people. The trick is to pull that off while remaining true to yourself", Harvard Business Review, December, 2005.

Doubt

As a leader begins to come to grips with his or her authentic leadership style, quite commonly, doubt and fear do begin to creep in. Conversations on topics like these start to run through the brain: "Can I do this?" and "Can I be authentic and still be credible?" and "If I bring my true self to this organization, will anyone want to follow me?" Being able to express your true personality, desires and vision and balance them with the culture of an organization is an advanced skill...one that truly separates a mediocre leader from a leader who can and will make a significant mark on a company, community or political group.

Coaching Questions:

- Why do your followers want to be led by you? If you don't know, ask them!

- Are you trying to emulate the leadership style of another leader? If so, why?

- If you were to allow yourself to become more authentic in your leadership, what would this look like? What would you change about your behaviors and decision making?

- When you consider becoming a more authentic leader, what doubts come up for you?

- How much are you allowing your followers to be authentic in their day in, day out work?

- Think of a skill, talent or creative part of yourself that was a big part of your childhood. How can you enhance your authentic leadership style by bringing that part of yourself back into your life as a leader?

- Think of a part of your roots or past that your team would benefit from by knowing about. How can you use that part of your life to establish common ground with your followers?

SEVENTEEN | Running

"**A**nna. What's up?" Mitch said to his wife curtly, after intercepting a call from his assistant.

"I'm fine, my day's going well. Thanks for asking. And how are you?"

"Look, I'm...that wasn't intentional..."

"It never is..." Anna said, halfway under her breath.

"What!?"

"Nothing. Look, I was just gonna ask if you'd stop and get some lamb chops or something on the way home. The boys want to barbeque and sit in the hot tub for a while tonight. Still too cold for the pool. They haven't seen much of you lately, you know," she added.

"I..." Mitch let go an exasperated sigh and tossed his glasses on top of the manila folder that glared at him from the desk. In it were details of a trade deal in Singapore that a team member had botched. The whole thing was threatening to go south...quickly. "I would love to. I just...I just don't know when I'll be home. That's all. Anna...I. I'll call."

"Right, of course. Like when Kyle waited up for you last week. Not to worry."

Silence.

"Anna, I'm..."

"Me, too." She cut him off and hung up.

Mitch heard himself let out a guttural sound, something between a growl and a moan, as he slammed down the receiver. It sounded like his father, and it sickened him.

Ten minutes later, his assistant buzzed again. "Mr. James? Kate Nelson for you."

"Shit!" he said out loud. "Um...yes. Give me ten seconds." He paced back and forth, talking out loud. "Get it together, Mitch. Golf course..." he said, trying to take himself to a calmer place. "I'm on the fucking golf course..." It wasn't working.

"Kate, how are you?" he said, with transparent sweetness.

"I'm fine. But assuming you haven't had any sort of emergency, I'm a little miffed at you. You missed our coaching call and didn't call to let me know what was going on before or after."

He launched into a laundry list of reasons why he had missed the appointment, the same one they'd been having at the same time on the same day every week for several months. "It wasn't intentional. These things happen, and I apologize. And I do have my environmental checklist! And the damn ficus tree is on it!" he laughed, trying to make light.

Kate wasn't deterred. "Look, I know that you have an assistant who tracks your appointments and can make calls for you. I get concerned when one of the top CEOs in the world handles his business this way. There's something to be learned here." She paused. "I want to know from you how missing our call today is significant to some of the challenges you're facing."

"Well, clearly it's a cause and effect relationship. Clearly! I mean, Maxy left because I didn't make this call to you." He punctuated his sarcasm with a cocky chuckle.

"Uh huh. Alright, Mitch. That's very funny," Kate said. "You're doing right now what you've done before with me. And I know that you do it with other people. I've got to admit that I feel myself sort of grinning on this end at your charming, disarming, dry humor..."

Mitch leaned back his chair and kicked his feet up on the desk.

"...so I know how powerful it is for you to slip into that behavior. But this is your **business** and this is your **life**," she continued. "So, I have a request for you. I want you to spend a few minutes this afternoon considering that question: why your missing the appointment and not calling is significant to your business and even to your personal relationships." She told him to call back at 5:00 for a short coaching call.

"I've been a naughty boy..." he said.

"I'm not name calling or judging, Mitch. I'm just calling your attention to a behavior that I have noticed and the lesson that can be learned here," Kate said, and Mitch asked her to repeat the question he was to consider. With that, his feet came off the desk.

He hesitated, tapping his pen on the desk, then reluctantly agreed. "It's yet another question that I'm just not convinced about. It feels like there's too much. The *authenticity* thing, the environment...I'm just not convinced that it's all relevant. And now you're saying *this-is-your-life*, as if some game show host is gonna pop out of my closet along with my third grade teacher or something!"

"Mitch, let's get one thing clear. I'm not giving up on you. I know that there are things that the Board wants for you and things that you want for yourself. And I am going to hold your feet to the fire. The only way that I won't continue getting in there and fighting for you is if you fire me. You can fire me. You can go to the Board and tell them *I'm not gonna do this any more.*"

"Touché," Mitch said after a few moments. "I will agree at this point to think about your question..." Mitch checked his calendar for 5:00 just as his assistant buzzed him again.

"Hold on, Kate..." he said. "Debbie, just...No, just tell them to wait. I'll be right there! Okay. Sorry about that, Kate," he continued, back on the phone. "Yes, 5:00 is free. I'll talk to you then. Now, I've gotta go put out another fire!"

Back in his office an hour later, the information on the Singapore deal looked like a half (and poorly) written script to him. He got the information; it just wasn't translating to a plan of action in his head, and he was still trying to figure out what to assign to whom since the team was no longer intact.

Just then, Graham popped his head in the door. "Hey, Mr. Outdamnstanding! Time for some cawfee talk?"

Mitch raised his hand. "Graham...not now."

"Whoa..." Graham said, ducking out just as quickly as he'd popped in.

"Great! Why don't you just go ahead and alienate everybody, asshole! You're on a roll! Why not?!" Mitch said to himself.

He walked over to the window. In an instant, he was overcome by the feeling that Kate's commitment to him, to "holding his feet to the fire," was more than he could offer himself. And definitely more than he could offer her; he hated the part of himself that couldn't—or wouldn't— reciprocate. His promise to keep the 5:00 appointment fell to the floor like yet another wilted, disdained ficus leaf. He turned around, grabbed his glasses from the desk and headed out of the office. He hadn't given a thought to where he was going. He was just going.

Running

In coaching over 800 leaders in the past, there is something that I have noticed on multiple occasions. When the heat gets turned up, or the leader begins to make a big change or a tough decision, he or she will often move into a cycle of what I call "running." Running shows up in many ways, including missing coaching calls, working on a long list of detailed activities so that they can appear "busy" (not having to work on what is most important) or using diversion tactics such as excuses, sarcasm, humor or blaming other people for the problems at hand or a lack of results.

Coaching Questions:

- Where, in your life as a leader, is the heat getting turned up?

- When you consider the heat getting turned up, what emotions are you feeling?

- What diversion tactics are you using to avoid having to make a big change or to address the challenges that are staring you in the face?

- As you consider the challenges that you are facing, whom are you blaming? Yourself or others? If you are blaming others, think again. What choices have you made or not made to lead to the challenges in front of you?

- When you consider "running," are you running *away* from something or *to* something? In either case, what is that *something*?

- If you are "running," what do you hope to achieve by running?

- What leadership qualities will be required of you in order to stop running and take full responsibility for what is going on in your life as a leader?

EIGHTEEN | Devastation

Mitch could feel every pounding beat of his heart. It felt to him that, with every thump, it was inching closer to his throat. He found himself swallowing hard and craning his neck continuously because loosening his tie did no good at all. As the light finally turned green, he beat the horn at a couple of hipster teens taking their time in the crosswalk. When they flipped him off, he beat the steering wheel and swerved around them.

His cell phone rang again. "Goddamnit! I'm on my way!" he shouted at Elizabeth's cell phone number on the screen. A hundred yards before he turned the corner and headed toward the office, he heard the blare of sirens, and the scene before him suddenly blurred as the sweat dripped into his eyes. It was even worse than he'd expected when Elizabeth had called him the first time, and what he'd imagined was bad enough.

He pulled the car to a screeching stop just behind the last fire truck. Getting out of the car and looking up, one thought ran on a loop through his head. *Holy shit...what have I done?* As if to outmaneuver the guilt that descended on him and made him shake from the inside out, he began to run. Bumping into onlookers and running around five fire trucks and three ambulances, he frantically scanned the crowd through the smoky air, heading straight for the blockade with no intention of letting it or the uniforms stop him.

"I need to get...!"

"Sir, you cannot pass!" the officer shouted back, cutting him off.

"You don't understand! I work here!"

"Not right now, you don't!" the brusque man grabbed Mitch by the arm.

"Let go of me!" Mitch shouted, jerking his arm free. "What happened?! Where is everyone?!"

"Sir, calm down. It appears that everyone got out of the building."

"Where are they, goddamnit?!"

"Mitch..." said a soft and shaky voice behind him.

"Leslie!" He spun around and hugged her. "Where is everyone?"

"This way," she said, turning to head back through the crowd. "Damn you, Mitch. We've been looking for you...we thought you were trapped inside. I finally found Elizabeth and she said she'd talked to you..." Her voice trailed off in residual tears.

"Is everyone okay?" he finally asked, eyeing a group of medics huddled around someone lying on the ground.

"Yes...I mean, yeah, I think everyone got out."

Mitch couldn't respond but didn't know whether to embrace the team or cower in shame when he looked up and saw each one of them. He could hardly bear the disappointment and confusion in their eyes.

"Mitch...where were you?" Elizabeth asked, shaken and angry.

Right on cue, another police car pulled up and blared its siren once to clear a path through the crowd on the wet street. Thankful for the distraction, Mitch steered everyone to the sidewalk just as a window exploded above, spraying shards of glass through the air. Everyone ran.

"This way!" Mitch led the way, running through the crowd and looking back to make sure everyone followed. Stephen took the rear, steering Leslie, Elizabeth, Jonathan and Graham. No one said a word as Mitch led them through the door and into the lobby of a motel across the street and adjacent to Global. There, an understanding doorman let the shaken group pass as he continued to watch the spectacle.

Graham put his arm around Leslie. Stephen stepped away, running a hand through his strangely disheveled hair and casting Mitch a sideways glance.

"What now?" Graham asked, calmly. It was the first thing he'd said to Mitch.

"I..." All he could do was shake his head. Suddenly he thought of the Board. "Has anyone talked to Bob?"

"Left him a message," Elizabeth said.

"I can try him again," Jonathan said, eager for something constructive to do.

"No...no, not yet. Here...come on, you guys," Mitch said, heading to a group of couches and chairs.

"Would you folks like some water?" the doorman called to them.

"Yes, yes...thank you," Mitch replied.

Leslie called her husband in hushed tones. Mitch thought of Anna and called her cell phone. He was surprised to feel grateful when the call went to voicemail. Leaving a disjointed message with his voice rising and falling randomly, he realized that his emotions were out of control. He was all over the place, and it scared him. He wondered how the team would respond to him.

"Kate...do you have a minute?"

"Actually, Mitch, I had plenty of time an hour and a half ago. You missed our call *again*. I need to have a discussion with you, but now I've got another..."

"Kate, I...I know...I'm...We've had a...a crisis. I could use...I need your support...to get grounded."

"Okay, what's happened?"

"A fire. There's been a fire...there's a fire now! It's...I mean the fire department's here. The police. It was fairly large. I don't know all the details... I...I feel like shit, Kate. I wasn't... I was at the..." Mitch stopped, trying to catch his breath. "I wasn't here...when it happened. I was gone, Kate."

"Okay, Mitch. I'm gonna just stop you right there for a minute. This is urgent. There's a lot of noise and commotion. Where are you right now?"

"I'm at a...we're, we're safe, just across the street... from the office. With the team. I got the team. We're here to get a plan of action together, but I am not thinking clearly. I need to get myself under control," he stammered.

"Okay, is there someplace you can go to get away from the chaos for just about five minutes or so?" she asked.

"I don't think that's such a good idea, Kate. I mean...I was *gone* when it happened. I left them. I don't think it's such a good idea for me to disappear *again*."

"My request is that you speak to someone on your team. Maybe Elizabeth. Let her know that you're just going to go down the hall to speak with me for only five minutes and that you'll be right back."

"Okay...okay...give me a few minutes, and I'll call you right back." Mitch looked out the window at the scene before him, squinted sharply, and then turned toward the team that now stood staring blankly at him.

Devastation

When a tragic event occurs, leaders are usually left baffled and shocked because, in the snap of a finger, life as they knew it ended or at least dramatically changed. People may feel tossed around by intense, unpredictable emotions...or—temporarily anyway—experience an awkward numbness.

As a leader, you must know that, when a disaster strikes, your followers will look directly and immediately to you for guidance. They don't want to ask who is in charge; there probably won't be time to ask that question. They'll need to know immediately what steps to take next. They will follow your lead and consider not only what you say, but also what you do. You will be their physical, emotional, and mental compass. It is critical that you remain calm in order to get cooperation and unity from your team so that smart, quick decisions can be made.

Coaching Questions:
Take the time to sit down and actually answer these questions. When a crisis hits, you will not have the time to think of these questions, so the best approach is to be prepared well in advance:

- Consider a time in the past when you were faced with a tragic event. What did you do to get grounded and focused?

- What practices can you implement quickly that will allow you to regain your composure and remain calm? (Pausing, deep breathing.)

- What steps can you take to get cooperation and unity from your team, even in the face of devastation?

- What strategies can you quickly implement that will prevent a breakdown in communication?

- What relief agencies from the community do you need on your side so that all stakeholders receive the support they need during a crisis?

NINETEEN | Breathing

"**M**itch, is that you?"

"Yes, yes, I called back as soon as I could."

"Where are you now?" Kate asked.

"Just down the hall from the team. Conference room," Mitch answered, feeling distracted.

"Mitch, I know that you feel like you need to be with your team and that there's a lot going on right now. But I'm so glad that you called me and I feel like this call is important. So, fill me in, please..."

Mitch paused, unsure of where to start, trying to sift through the images flashing through his mind. "I...it was probably 1:00 or so. One thing after another..." Mitch said, rattling off the disjointed list of the day's annoyances. "I just...I'd had enough. Just sort of snapped, grabbed my glasses, and left. I was gone before I even realized I was leaving. I needed to...I don't know...clear my head.

"I was sitting there at the park eatin' my damn cookie..." Mitch went on, shaking his head in disgust at himself. "The phone rang. It was Elizabeth. She was...crying...in a panic. There was smoke pouring through the building, coming maybe from the back, the boiler room. Everybody had to be evacuated from the building. We don't know the extent of the damage, but there was a fire...well, you know that," Mitch paused, and as he looked toward the building again, a wave of nostalgia rushed over him, catching him completely off guard. "Um, I'm still putting this together in my head...I just got some of the details from the team right before I called you back."

Mitch noticed that the smoke was still floating in the air but no longer billowing out of any and all openings. He cringed at the sight. "Everyone got out...thank God! Three people had to be taken to the hospital. Smoke inhalation, anxiety, I'm not sure, but no burns or injuries. And...I don't know...I'm just eyeballing it, but I'd say we lost maybe a quarter of the building. Seems to be going out. But," he said, turning away from the window and pacing, "By the time I got here it was utter pandemonium. I just...I don't know what to do. I just can't friggin' believe it, Kate. I feel so *incredibly* guilty..."

Kate interrupted him there. "Mitch, this crisis is something that most leaders don't ever think they'll have to go through. I know it's almost impossible to take it all in right now, but you told me when you called that you needed my help to get grounded. I think that's a good idea." Asking him to find a comfortable place to sit, she took the reigns, and Mitch offered no resistance as she led him into a breathing exercise. "Go ahead and breathe in and out very deeply and consciously ten times." He did. "How are you now?" she asked.

"Well, a little better, but still in a panic."

"I know. And this is no time for an in-depth coaching call, but I wanted to start to get your feet back on the ground. I'm just going to ask you a series of questions, and the goal is to be as brief, calm and clear as possible. First, you mentioned that three people had been hospitalized. What do you need to do to address that situation?"

He stammered a bit. "Um...have someone call...Elizabeth maybe."

"Continue. I'm taking notes as we speak, Mitch, to help give you an action plan."

"I will need to contact the employees who have been hospitalized...oh...and their families. Kate, I really feel like I need to get back to my team."

She agreed. "But I just want to talk with you for a few more minutes. It's extremely important that you go back to your team as calm and centered as possible...because they will be following your emotional lead. If you are panicked, they are going to be panicked. So, are you willing to work with me for 3 or 4 more minutes?"

"Yes. Okay."

"Mitch, where is the team?"

"Um, the lobby. They're in the lobby. Except for Stephen. He was gonna go out and try to get some information from the authorities," he answered.

"And what was your intention in bringing the team to the hotel?"

"Well, to give us a place to think away from the chaos and...I just thought it was important to get away from...it's just pandemonium over there. I could not think clearly."

"And the employees are outside on the streets?" Kate asked.

Mitch explained that most of them were, yes, and that some had gone home.

"Does your company have a Crisis and Communication Plan?"

"Um..." he paused, retracing some steps in his brain. "Yes, yes, of course."

"And where is the plan?"

"*Shit!*" Mitch said, rattling off several other expletives and punching the top of his thigh with his fist when he realized that it was on his computer hard drive.

"And is your computer system backed up remotely?" Kate asked coolly, keeping him focused.

He was quiet for a moment. "Oh! Yes! Yes, it is!"

"It's okay, everything's gonna be okay. Just continue to breathe," she said. "And who can take care of calling the company that handles that service for you?"

"Alan. No! Shit! Not Alan, he's gone. Um...Leslie. Leslie can do that."

Kate took further notes and kept him on course. "Alright, the next steps are very important, because following your Crisis and Communication Plan is going to be critical. What are your first steps with that plan?"

He determined that getting in touch with Bob and the Board was key.

"They don't know about the fire?" Kate asked, surprised.

"Well, I'm sure they do by now, but I wasn't the one who made the call," he said, and Kate agreed that getting to Bob was essential.

"Now then, how do you want to respond to the team and the employees? More precisely, how do you want them to respond to you in this crisis?"

"Well," Mitch said, "Calmly. I want them to know that we have a plan, that everything will be okay, that we're acting swiftly..."

"And what do you think is going on in their minds right now?" Kate asked.

"'What the hell are we gonna do?!' I'm wondering the same thing."

Kate clarified. "Mitch, I'm sure most of them already realize that they've lost personal possessions. They're probably wondering if the company will survive and worrying about what they'll do when they wake up in the morning...if they will still have a job. They're going to have a lot of questions. So, what do you do as their leader to make sure that their questions get answered?"

"I need to be clear, succinct...just...damn it! I don't know what the *fuck* to tell them!" He paced and looked out the window.

Kate reminded him that he didn't know because he didn't have the necessary tools yet. That is, he'd know how to proceed once he had a copy of the Crisis and Communication Plan and had talked to Bob. "From where I'm standing as a coach, your job right now is to let your team and your employees know that you'll be taking the steps spelled out in the Plan and briefing them along the way. It's important to balance your communication and action steps with all of the emotions that you're feeling...because those emotions will be unbalanced right now... and—whether you realize it or not—you will set the emotional tone for everyone else, Mitch. Let them know that you will be communicating with them consistently over the next few hours because they will be looking to you for answers."

"Okay. I can do that. I just don't know about the media. They're swarming like locusts," Mitch said.

"So, how do you handle that?"

"No comment! Seriously, I need to talk to the Board first, see what they want who to say when about what, blah, blah, blah...and..." Mitch slowed, sounding like his voice was twisting inside his chest. "...and I wasn't even in the building, Kate..."

"Mitch, I certainly understand your conflicted feelings, but let's stay focused so you can move calmly and quickly. And the Board will lay down the guidelines for your communications and theirs. Mitch, how are you feeling now?"

"Well...really, really guilty..."

That was a given, but Kate didn't go there. She told him they could schedule a coaching call in the next several days and promptly steered him back on course. "What do you think your team, your employees and the Board need from you right now?"

"I...I think they just really need me to step up. To really take charge, delegate effectively. Get some professionals down here if anyone's really having a hard time. I need to create a plan...be the point man..." Mitch grew silent without realizing it as he looked out the window and saw something that he never expected.

It was Stephen. Stephen, of all people, was milling about in the crowd. With rumpled hair, loosened tie and no jacket, with shirt-sleeves rolled up, he was making the rounds to employees with one of the housekeeping staff, an elderly woman, hovering close to him. Of course, Mitch couldn't hear a word he said, but he didn't need to. Suddenly, the brawny CFO was waving his arms in the air. Mitch looked in the same direction and saw a cab approaching. When it pulled up, Stephen opened his wallet, gave the driver a wad of cash, helped the woman inside, and waved them on their way with a smile.

"Mitch?"

"Uh, yeah. Yeah, I'm here," he said, clearing his throat to keep his voice from wavering. "Um...people. As we move through this, I need to put people first. And they need to see me calm, controlled, and confident because...because that's what they'll respond well to. It's what they need."

"Okay," Kate said. With that, she asked him to reiterate his immediate plan of action. Mitch had it down and rattled off his list: first, call Bob; second, have Leslie contact the remote facility and email the Crisis and Communication plan to his BlackBerry; third, talk openly with the team and assure them that the Plan is in place and will be carried out swiftly; fourth, communicate the same thing to the employees; fifth, have Elizabeth contact the hospitalized employees and then get in touch with each of them personally—along with their families—over the next 24 hours. He added that he'd have Graham and Jonathan help him with the logistics of a temporary office space. And Stephen...Stephen would be "instrumental in supporting employees," he concluded, unable to take his eyes off of him.

"Mitch, last but not least, I want to tell you that I am truly saddened by all of this. I'm here for you if you need me, Mitch, and I have been from the start."

Still looking out on the street, he knew he believed her. For the first time, he really believed her.

Breathing

The events of September 11 have forever changed our world, calling leaders from all walks of life to look seriously at how to lead during a crisis. Leaders never expect something tragic to happen to them, yet the reality is that, as a leader, it is critically important to always be prepared for crises, both small and large. There are four main areas that are important to consider during a crisis: 1) Maintaining visibility; 2) Communicating clearly, both verbally and in writing; 3) Remaining emotionally calm, centered and focused; and 4) Gathering perspective from key leaders in the organization to create a plan for the next steps.

Coaching Questions:
In order to prepare your company for a crisis, you will want to make sure that these questions have been addressed:

- Do you have a crisis plan? If not, what steps will you need to take today to develop one for your organization?

- What steps can you take to increase your visibility during a crisis?

- What steps can you take to increase and enhance your face-to-face communication skills, both verbal and written?

- What emotions do you want your team to experience from you? What types of emotions do you want to create around you?

- Who are the main leaders in your organization whom you will want to gather in order to gain perspective and make an action plan for next steps?

- What do you most want to prevent? (Chaos, hysteria, rumors.)

- How will you address the media?

- How will you address key stakeholders of the organization?

TWENTY | Taking Command

"**A**re you *kidding* me?" Elizabeth said with a tone that bordered on contempt.

Mitch, the team, Bob and a couple of the other Board members stood in the threshold of the temporary office space that Global would be moving into; Maureen and Charles had been Board members since before Bob had even joined Global. Mitch figured that their presence was somewhat of a formality, but he knew that they were both relatively supportive of him, so he appreciated Bob's bringing them into the loop.

The downtown space was small, very small relative to the office. It was another building that the company owned and used for storage and international meetings and the like. Mitch honestly couldn't imagine how they'd manage, but the subject wasn't open for debate. It was the only realistic alternative.

Bob stood surveying the team's reaction with one arm crossed over his chest while the opposite hand rubbed his chin. Elizabeth gave a slight huff and started to walk off on her own to look around.

Mitch scrambled to the front and turned to face everyone while he talked. "Look, I'd...I'd like to have everyone stay gathered here for a min..."

His COO ignored him. "Excuse me," he called in her direction. "Elizabeth..." he said, but it was more of a question than a beckon. She continued, raising her hand, indicating that she'd be there when she decided to be. Standing there between the group and the defector, Mitch heard in his head echoes of the comments everyone had made about his leadership during the 360-feedback. He could feel Leslie's well-meaning but almost condescending concern creeping up on his back, but he shook it off.

"Elizabeth!" he called, firmly but not disrespectfully. She turned around and shot him a look that said, *You talkin' to me?*

The adrenaline was palpable. "Please join us, Elizabeth," Mitch continued in the same tone.

She glanced from him to the group and back again, finding no sign of support. She slowly walked back over to the edge of the group. Mitch couldn't help but think of *Cool Hand Luke*. In his head he was saying, "What we've got here is a failure to communicate," as he did with a certain levity to his boys over issues of homework or chores. This, though, was no time for levity, and he didn't need to lean on any clever lines.

With a subtle, affirmative nod from Bob, Mitch realized that he actually had everyone's attention, but his heart was pounding so hard, he could hardly speak. He'd been on the phone with everyone over the weekend, but this was different. Everyone waited. "This...this is hard. I know that only two days have passed since the fire. Yes, we've had a couple of resignations in different departments, but we have got to pull ourselves back together. The space is small, yes, but we can do this. We need this new office up and running by Friday. In fact, *on* Friday, all of the employees—except the ones that can telecommute—will be here. We're here today to make a plan of action. First and foremost..."

"...is the fact that you are a hypocrite, Mitchell James." It was Elizabeth again.

"Hey, whoa!" Jonathan said, but the comment fell on deaf ears.

"Pull ourselves *back* together?" she continued. "Is that what you said? We can't pull ourselves *back* to something that we never really were. Sure, the world sees us as one of the best, but behind the brick and mortar, we're just running around bumping into walls. And we weren't *together* when the fire happened, now were we? Well, some of us were, but the captain of this ship jumped over board yet again that day."

"Elizabeth, please. Let me..."

"And since the captain doesn't communicate with the first-mate—that would be me..." she said, as if informing the rest of the team, and getting louder with each word, "We are completely lost at sea!" She grew quiet as her grief surfaced. "I don't see how we'll ever get out of this..."

"This kind of crisis can bring us *together*..." Leslie said, starting to answer for Mitch.

"No, Leslie. She's right," he interrupted. Leslie was shocked. Stephen shifted uncomfortably. "I don't want to make light of this situation. It's dire. Absolutely. And I know...I know that I've let you all down...in more ways than I'm probably even aware. I...I don't know how to say this...it sounds so..." He felt the urge to pace, but forced himself to stand firm and look squarely at the eyes that were on him. "Nothing I can say will change what I've done or not done or make what's happened any easier. But I can tell you this much with absolute certainty: I won't pretend to understand how this whole thing is playing out for any of us, but I know—now more than ever—that I am *not* going anywhere. My commitment to this company..." He paused to clarify and caught Graham's eye. "My commitment to all of *you*...to *each* of you is stronger than ever."

Elizabeth rolled her eyes. "It's the same old song and..."

"Your attitude is not helping here, Elizabeth!" said Leslie, coming as close to a yell as she ever had with her colleagues. With that, the call was out, and the two fired several rounds.

"As COO, I am entitled...!"

"There is no entitlement...!"

"Look who's talking!" Elizabeth shouted back. "You seem to feel entitled to speak for our CEO half the..."

"I speak because I love this..."

"Ladies, ladies..." Stephen said, sounding genteel even in argument. "Look, none of us is happy..."

"Stephen, you wouldn't know happy if it..." Leslie was showing some edge.

"Shut the hell up and let Mitch speak!" Jonathan chimed in.

"I need a cigarette..." Maureen said in disgust, and headed out the door.

"Indoor voices, kids, and watch your language," Graham piped up, somewhat amused at the colors that were showing.

"Don't be condescending, Graham," Stephen warned, as Charles added, "He's right! You sound like a bunch of school kids!"

"The important thing is to remember that we're a team!" Leslie said, practically pleading.

"Listen!" Elizabeth yelled. "I, for one, will *not* hold hands and go down with a sinking ship!"

"We will *not* go down!" All heads turned in Mitch's direction. He was practically shaking. A mild sweat dampened his hair and held it away from his face after he'd run his hand through it. "You heard me. We will *not*...go...down! If any of you wants to leave, jump now and swim for shore...because the rest of us are gonna work our asses off to get back afloat. Having said that, I also have to say that I need you all. We've got clients to call, accounts to nurture. We can't miss a beat." He took off his jacket and tossed it on the floor. Everyone watched quietly and exchanged glances as he unbuttoned his cuffs and rolled his sleeves up. Elizabeth bit her lip. "I need the white board and a pen." Graham was on the task. "I also need some chairs. In a circle. So we can brainstorm. Now. And don't get too comfortable in your chairs...you'll each have your turn at the board. I want to hear from every last one of you."

Stephen looked around and then went to gather the chairs. Jonathan followed.

Bob smiled ever so slightly at Charles, as if to say *I told you so.*

As Graham set the white board next to Mitch, he said under his breath, "Outdamnstanding, Grasshopper..."

"This place is amazing," Kate said. They sat at a café, both a little mesmerized by the open, airy décor and the self-contained fountain-waterfall in the center of the room. It looked as if the building had sprouted up naturally around the little oasis that seemed to rise from an open space in the earth.

"Yeah," Mitch said, sipping his coffee, relieved that Kate wasn't pressing him for information. They hadn't spoken in awhile; she'd given him time and space to find his feet after the fire. "How long...how long do you think it takes for flowing water to smooth stones like that? You know, all of those rough edges..."

"Rough edges. Hmm...I guess some are rougher than others. But it must be the continual flow that does it. You know, the focus, the direction of the current."

Mitch smiled. "Yeah, persistence does wonders, eh? But sometimes change comes best in swift doses."

"Does it?" Kate asked.

Mitch nodded and finally looked directly at her. "Yes. You know me, Kate. For so long, I'd been dancing around all of my so-what questions. All of my defenses, the song and dance routines, the ol' shuck and jive. You called me out on 'em every time. The whole act was wearing on me, but I just kept it alive. And then came the fire to raze it all. Poof...no more façade."

"I want to get to the fire, but tell me about water first. I see you watching it... almost admiring it. You are here across from me, but you seem far away. What does it mean to you?"

Mitch smiled a big smile. "Well, it makes me nostalgic. When I was kid, we spent time at this resort-like area with cabins right on a lake. Of course, as I got older, I managed to talk Dad into letting me use the 8mm camera. He spent a lot of time working, even when we were on vacation, so I think he agreed just to get me out of his hair. Anyway, I shot a lot of great footage there, on the lake. Normally, I wanted to script everything, call the shots. When we were at the lake, though, I liked to get candid shots of my family and random strangers—people relaxed and enjoying life. So, being by the water was just...the absolute joy of creating and being, without thoughts of what it all meant. People were the center of everything then. Relationships...how they looked and felt. How I perceived them... So, I guess that's what the water reminds me of. Relationships."

He told Kate that he'd been to this café a dozen or more times and had always found the waterfall hokey before today. "But I guess the fire—don't laugh...this sounds so dramatic—separated the dross from the gold, you know. Purification. It gave me room for those so-what questions to rise to the surface. You want to be the top international trade corporation in the world? So what? You're the CEO for the company? So what? Top business people around the globe know your name? So what?"

Kate sat back and gave him room to continue.

"I've had other questions on my mind. What if someone had been hurt in the fire? What if someone had died? I wrestle with overwhelming guilt, as is. I don't think I could have forgiven myself, Kate." He looked at the water and back again. "It's about people. About relationships. About making a difference. These things have become so clear to me.

"I know this isn't therapy, but I have to tell you that leading this company had always felt so empty to me. I hated that feeling...and I was so busy running from it that I didn't even know how to slow down long enough to see where the meaning really was...until I was forced to slow down...to stop even. And..." Mitch paused, shaking his head in sheer wonder. Since that day, he had played over and over again in his head the vision of Stephen helping the woman in the street. "...I can't explain to you how I came to see it, but those bottom-line, so-what questions are answered only in the context of relationships. It's the people that give meaning to those answers."

"Mitch, you've assimilated so many changes and emotions so quickly. That's a skill of great leadership," Kate said. "I saw the glimmer of that skill in you when you called me back during the fire. You immediately began to multi-task your way through everything that had landed before you." She could see that he was still struggling with one particular emotion, though. "Tell me about the guilt."

Mitch explained that, while intellectually he realized he most likely couldn't have prevented the fire even if he had been in the building, he still resented himself for having cut out of work once again. "Worse yet, I wonder...what if I had been there, and not stepped up? What if I'd been there and still failed everyone? I like to think that I would have rallied everyone and led them heroically to safety. But maybe I wouldn't have. I own that possibility."

"Specifically, though...hmm...I know this may sound like an odd question, but how has the guilt served you to this point?"

Mitch recalled the avoidance he'd mentioned earlier. "Well, if I'm sitting around pitying myself and being preoccupied with beating myself up, I don't have to do anything constructive."

"Where else in your life have you felt that kind of guilt?"

"Hold that thought," he answered, getting up for a refill of coffee. Sitting back down, he copped to some more avoidance, admitting that, until the fire, he'd never told Anna about the coaching, the alter-ego business/comedy club trips, or his film-school regrets, or his enduring thoughts of Rory. "That was the hardest part...Rory. Anna went a little ballistic, until I explained that it wasn't romantic, passionate regrets. It was envy of her strength to choose the life she really wanted, but that—despite those feelings—there's nowhere else I would rather be today than there with Anna and...our sons," Mitch said, getting a little breathy but forcing himself to recover. "And when I told her that—no matter what's going on in my life—she *always* comes first, she cried, and it occurred to me that I'd never said those words to her before."

"Mitch, I have to say that you sound like a different person than the one I've been coaching for the last six months." Commenting on his remarkable openness, she asked him what had scared him so much about being honest with his wife.

That question called for a long sigh before the response. "I was afraid she'd take the same route as my father...belittle me and be ashamed of my interests. But she didn't. It was so much easier to be candid than I thought it'd be!" While he was on a roll, he got a little more transparent with Kate, too.

"I want to apologize here and now to you, too, Kate, for missing those three coaching calls. There's just...there's something so intuitive and magical about the way you work, and it scared me. Intimidated me. When you turned up the heat on me, it was more comfortable for me to default to my M.O. and run the way I've been running from my own truth for decades now. I see now that it's always been so easy for me to run...responsibilities, discomfort, relationships. Ironically, it was the literal heat—the fire—that halted me."

"Top leaders like you, Mitch, require challenge to really grow; it wouldn't have served you for me to coach you at a level that was comfortable and convenient for you." She echoed his sentiment about his tendency to run, saying that his procrastination on the manifesto had set off the tumbling dominos of running within this coaching process.

"Yes. I noticed the repeating pattern of running. At every step," Kate continued, "I tried to up the ante, increase the challenge a bit to see what would happen in the running pattern: would you run harder or do an about face? I see another pattern, too, Mitch. You've not only been running; as you already mentioned, you've been pretty good at hiding your truth from the people closest to you. If—like you said—you began hiding your creativity as a child, then it was easy to fall into that pattern as an adult. The human brain is programmed to repeat patterns until something happens to break them. So, as much as I hate that the fire happened, I believe that it did *interrupt* your behavior patterns of running and hiding. I say *interrupt*. Time will tell whether or not you *choose* to actually *break* the patterns of running and hiding. You're saying that the fire caused a change in your patterns. I can point you to numerous studies that indicate that catastrophic events are instruments of *real, lasting* change."

It was all making sense to Mitch. Kate continued, stressing the importance of consciously creating new grooves in his thought patterns. Mitch thought back to how he'd felt himself wanting to pace and stall in front of the team the first day at the temporary space. He told Kate how he'd caught himself in another avoidance maneuver and chosen an alternate path, standing squarely and addressing the team and Board. "Yes, that's exactly the kind of thing I'm talking about," she said. "You'll learn to create new behaviors. With repetition, they'll become your new default settings!"

"Everything you're saying is right on the money. It's just...the overwhelm!" he said, resting his forehead on his hands before meeting Kate's eyes again.

"Tell me about that overwhelm. What are you feeling?"

"Well, in a nutshell—defense mechanisms are gone...everything else is rushing in! Let's see…" He detailed all of the new logistics and responsibilities of rebuilding and redesigning the office. "The Board looks at me and says 'what do you want?'…and I have no idea. Add to that the fact that we're now in a space one-fourth the size of the old building. We're practically on top of one another. Thank goodness some people can telecommute!" On the upside, he said, was the fact that work was being expedited because there was no lag time between departments. "Mary in graphics starts formatting before we hand her a report because she overhears everything we're saying from the get-go! It's really kind of fascinating. There's just…there's a lightness now that's never been there before."

Kate leaned up on the table. "Correct me if I'm wrong, but it sounds like Global is truly up and running again, maybe not with ultimate efficiency, but still with a good degree of effectiveness. Is that right?"

Mitch agreed, saying that communicating clearly with clients—letting them know that their needs would be met despite the atmosphere of change—was the tallest order. "I'd say we're operating at about 95%. We probably could've lost a few clients at first, but we really pulled it together and retained everyone. We're even courting a couple of potential clients."

The biggest challenge, he said, was the building. "It's structurally sound. Now I just have to decide how to build on that structure. A blank canvas is overwhelming…and that's what our office is right now."

"Well, let me remind you of an old expression…*you eat an elephant one bite at a time.* Fortunately, you have a team of very high-achieving people, so you'll be taking bigger bites—and more of them—more quickly." Kate shared the sense of calm and faith she felt in Mitch, his team, and the Board in moving ahead. "Speaking of people, my gut is telling me that I should share one of my biases with you. Any time I work with someone who is going to be redesigning, what I see is a great opportunity to tell a story. You, Mitch, have the opportunity to tell the world a story about your company and its people by the way you choose to redesign your building. And I'm not talking about great trade negotiations or international dealings. Let me ask you something. What is it that really carries a story or film?"

"Well, there has to be a great plot structure, but even more than that, it comes down to the characters...to engaging, multi-dimensional characters...the kind that leap off the page or screen," Mitch answered.

"Exactly. So, what is it that brings the story of Global Trade Management to life?" Kate said, and Mitch could hear the smile in her voice.

"Ah, yes...the people. It's about the people..."

Kate agreed that people determine the character of a business, or any organization or group, for that matter. That character should drive the design. "To get down to what the people are all about, I like to start with values...core values, the things that matter most. So let me take you back in time. Describe for me what was so important about that childhood time in your life when you were so actively engaged in your films, in being creative."

"Wow...well, it was the excitement of creating something from nothing. Of being at the helm of telling a story...ah..." Mitch said, with a slight laugh. "I see where you're going with this. I loved to get to tell a story and see how people reacted to it...I don't think I was aware of it then, but looking back, I see that I felt such joy in affecting positive emotions in people, of taking them on a journey."

"And when you were directing these films, you had a team with you...helpers?"

"Yes, absolutely! I had several loyal friends...and I loved bringing them along in the process to the point that they were completely on board with me. You know, they would come to share my vision, but it was a give and take. I learned from them, too. And they loved it! Even when I was bossy, we had a ball..."

"Would you say that you felt like your *authentic* self then...I know it's the A-word..." Kate concluded jokingly.

"In retrospect, yeah. I didn't have to think about doing what felt like the real me. I just did it. And, you know...never thought I'd say this...the filmmaking was the *vehicle* for authenticity, how I expressed it. I still know what my truth is. Been running from it for a long time, but it's still there. And it's really about transformation...about nurturing the talent—my own and that of others—and creating something bigger than ourselves. I can't believe how clear that's become to me.

"And you know," Mitch continued, "after my friends and I made the first few films, we barely even had to speak with each other to communicate...we could practically speak in shorthand. We just had this synergy, which I guess really came down to trust."

Mitch noticed the sound of the water for the first time in at least thirty minutes. Kate took the conversation a little deeper, taking brief notes on a small pad she held on her lap.

"Now tell me about a time in your life when things weren't going so well for you."

Mitch went immediately to college, to his breakup with Rory.

"What was missing for you then?" Kate asked.

"What do you mean?"

"A minute ago, you mentioned the synergy, the connections you felt with everything and everyone in your zone. What connections were missing at this time?"

"I...it was confusing. Didn't feel like truth. I'd come to feel like I was going through the motions, and I didn't understand why. I just knew that my life was going in a different direction...and that she wouldn't be willing to come with me... and I didn't know how to go with her. We hit a crossroads. I felt like I was losing my best friend. I knew that, if I was going to go out in the big bad world and live up to the expectations I felt, I was goin' it alone. I was losing my base...my..."

Mitch waved his hand as if reaching for something. "What is it?...my stone...my *touchstone*...It was gone...It sucked..."

Mitch was quiet for a moment, thinking. "There was no team. It was just me trying to guess at what was going to create this 'me' that I perceived others wanted me to be."

"Mitch, for the last six months, every time we've spoken, I've taken notes. There are certain words that you've used with increasing consistency, and I've circled them. Here," she said, ripping a blank sheet of her paper out for him, "write these down as I read them off and tell me if they make sense for you. The first one is **truth**. The second is **trust**. The third is **team**. The fourth is **talent**. The fifth is **transformation**. The sixth is actually a new one, but it's powerful... **touchstone**. When you said that word it struck a chord with me because a touch-stone is generally regarded as symbolic of a high standard or of being grounded in something very rich and real. So, how do those words strike you?"

Mitch started laughing. "Well, they all start with T. I must've been watching a lot of Sesame Street on the T-theme days in my formative years..."

"You could be on to something there," Kate laughed too, getting up for another cup of java. "Seriously," she continued, sitting down again, "You used other words like *creativity* and *inspiration*, but always in reference to a bigger process, to the *transformation* that you felt in creating your films and the *transformation* you've spoken of in terms of what happens when you watch an engaging film."

Mitch nodded in complete agreement, saying that there was a powerful message in each of the words. "When I think of transformation in terms of my life now, I ask myself, how is Global going to show up in the world? How will we transform our leadership, our creativity, our collaboration into something huge that affects not only our internal environment...but also the world in a positive way?"

"How do you see that happening?"

"Wow..." Mitch stammered for a moment. "The word legacy comes to mind... what we leave behind." He launched into a long list of attainable ideals: scholarships, foundations, charitable contributions and grants to similarly aligned organizations. "Those things can become real by leveraging not only our financial but also our human capital and resources. I even see offering people sabbaticals to spend six months or a year doing *meaningful work* that we would fund."

"Mitch, you are really inspiring me in this conversation. The ideals that you're creating around truth, authenticity and creativity will create a momentum that Global has not experienced before. You'll actually change the way that work is done. When people are allowed to do their work from a place of truth, your lead on that issue will be noticed by other people in the business world."

He pondered that idea without comment.

"You have the ability, the opportunity to change the way that work is done around the world, Mitch."

"Leading by example," he said. "You know, I think that the ability to lead that way all comes down to one word...truth...it's the most powerful for me."

"How so?"

"It's about that authenticity and transparency. And not just for me. For every team member, employee, client, and stakeholder that we serve—to be able to be co-leaders in a sort of...bigger vision. A vision that goes beyond the *work* itself to serve people. That can only happen, I see now, when everyone operates from their own truth. And where there's truth, there can be disagreement without judgment because we're all inspired by the same core values." Mitch was on a roll, spouting ideas as they came to him. He suddenly realized that those core values would be reflected in hiring processes and new contracts, as Global would attract like-minded people. "Truth will mean that we can even turn away work that's not aligned with us, without us questioning or second guessing ourselves!"

"How do you feel about that?"

"I say bring it on!" Mitch said. "I don't know how the Board will feel..." he added, laughing.

"What about letting go of current work that's not aligned with your core values?"

Mitch answered that that move would be a tougher sell, but one that would get easier with each passing day, as the core values became further instilled in every aspect of Global.

Kate reinforced the fact that the process of integrating core values takes time. "But once everyone—inside the company walls and outside of them—is aligned, the floodgates open, bringing more work than you can handle because you poise yourself so attractively in the marketplace. How does that sound?"

"Fantastic. We'll be like a lighthouse," Mitch said. "A guiding light in the darkness. And folks can either step onto the solid foundation that we'll offer, step off of it or sail on by altogether." He added that he probably already knew of a handful of people and accounts that would do so. "And that's just fine, because that'll make more room for those who reflect the truth."

The lighthouse idea made Mitch think of water again, and he noticed the trickling sound of the waterfall. He was lost in thought for a few minutes, and Kate didn't interrupt him. "You know," he said, sitting up straighter, "It just hit me that I want the—I don't know—the abundance and the power and the fluidity of water reflected in those t-words...in our core values. Water is ever-changing, unstoppable, dynamic."

"Brilliant, Mitch. Truly brilliant."

Taking Command

As their leader, followers will look to you during a time of crisis for direction, strength and unwavering confidence. They **want** to know that you are willing and able to step up and take command, even when the heat is on. Leading through crisis means taking command and getting your team aligned in the direction of the next steps that will either make or break your success. Doing so takes guts and a willingness to fail or make an unpopular decision because you know that, in the end, you are using your best judgment to make the most beneficial decisions for every stakeholder in your company, community or organization.

Take an honest look at yourself. How willing are you to step up and call the shots 100% when all eyes are on you and the stakes are high? If you are not willing to boldly *take command*—make an unpopular decision, get people moving, take a risk—during a crisis, what is holding you back? And why?

Coaching Questions:

- What skills will you use to get your team on board during a transition, crisis or turning point in your company?

- On a scale of 1-10, how willing are you to make an unpopular decision during a turning point for your company, community, family or organization, because you know in your heart that it's best for the majority of your stakeholders?

- Revisit your core values from earlier in the book. Decide how you will use them as a foundation for decision making during a crisis.

- As you take command during a crisis, what behaviors will you not tolerate in your team? (Constant complaining, gossip, objections without solutions.) How will you let team members know when they have crossed the line, and what positive alternative behaviors will you offer them?

BONUS: In an effort to assist you in **Taking Command,** Writers of the Round Table Inc., is inviting *Edge* readers to participate in a teleclass called *Taking Command: How to determine your Core Values and use them to raise your stakes!* For more information, visit http://www.Edge-Book.com/bonus.

TWENTY ONE | Redesigning

Mitch stood there looking out on the lake, listening to the water lap, lap, lap upon the shore. An unfamiliar sense of calm crept up from the soles of his feet to the top of his head. Again, he felt the urge to pace, but he forced himself to stand still with the early afternoon sun on his face, a slight breeze at the back of his neck and an intentionally agenda-less hour or two before him. He knew that he had felt this way long, long ago, and wondered just how he'd developed such a tolerance for the endless chatter that had filled his head in the interim.

He'd made sure to be the first one to arrive at the cabin. At the end of his last meeting with Kate, she'd taken Mitch's musings about creative-time with the team and suggested that he consider an extended off-site weekend for the purpose of brainstorming about the redesign for the building. "Yes...somewhere near the water," Mitch had replied quickly, and then invited Kate to join them. Join them, she would.

For a moment, Mitch felt a pang of something and thought of the boys and Anna. Then he realized it was simply the ache to spend time like this with them, instead of taking more of the separate vacations that had become part and par-cel of their family life, as it were. He leaned down to pick up a small stone and skipped it across the water. Taking out his cell phone, he snapped a shot of the lake and tree-lined shore, and sent it to Anna's phone, with the message, "Our upcoming family vacation."

Just as he was returning from a walk around the shore, he heard Kate pulling into the gravel driveway. "Levi's and a t-shirt! I like it!" she said, getting out of the car with a smile. They'd planned to meet an hour before the rest of the group arrived to go over some of the concepts that Mitch planned to address through the course of the weekend.

"Yes, it's my alter ego at its finest! You dress down well yourself!" he said, grabbing her bag and heading toward the covered front porch of the large cabin that Global had rented for the occasion. Kate replied that any excuse for cargo pants was good enough for her.

"Gorgeous! Good choice on this place," Kate said as they took seats in weathered wicker chairs to admire the view before heading inside. "This is a big step, Mitch. How are you feeling?"

He nodded for a minute and rested his elbows on his knees. "Good. Scared. Good n' scared!" he said with a laugh. "No, I...this getaway is just what we need. Besides, I'm looking forward to seeing everyone out-of-costume, so to speak!"

One after another, cars pulled in. First, came Bob, with Maureen and Charles in the Lincoln Town Car. Bob was all smiles and handshakes. Mitch had to struggle with the awkwardness of thinking that his Chairman was dressed like a JC Penney ad. Maureen and Charles were hardly as casual or comfortable. Mitch couldn't help but assume that Maureen, in particular, would be much more at home at the country club with a martini and a Virginia Slim.

Next came Stephen in the Benz, followed by Elizabeth in the Lexus. Mitch took a doubletake—and noticed that everyone else did, too—when she got out wearing brilliant orange gauze pants, a billowy blouse and flat leather sandals; it was a far cry from the conservative buttoned-up look that she favored from nine to five. The rest of the group was making slightly awkward small talk on the front porch when Jonathan pulled in and went immediately to the trunk of his BMW to haul out a large ice chest.

"I thought Graham was bringing the rest of the vittles..." Mitch called, running over to help him.

"Yeah, this is his. He asked me to bring it for some reason. Said he wouldn't have room or something, which makes no sense at all. Whatever."

The group convened around the kitchen island and poured tall glasses of lemonade and laid out the cheese and crackers. Jonathan wandered off to check out the wide screen TV and stereo surround-sound system. All heads turned toward the window when the thundering roar of a motorcycle approached. When someone let go a boisterous "Wooohooooo!" from the proximity of the driveway, everyone headed to the front porch.

"What the hell?" Stephen said, and Maureen looked terrified, grabbing Bob's arm.

Mitch was about to yell *May I help you?!* when the first helmet came off. Everyone was speechless. It was Graham, clad in a leather jacket with chaps over his Calvin Klein jeans on the back of a motorcycle, waving his red bandana and calling out something that resembled a victory cry. The driver's helmet came off next. It was Leslie, donning leather from head to toe.

"Oh my God!" said Mitch.

"You've got to be kidding me..." Elizabeth mumbled.

It called for another double take all around when Bob started to clap and let out the kind of ear-piercing whistle you'd hear at a parade or a rodeo. Maureen held a weathered hand lightly over her heart and looked away.

"Well, I'll be damned!" Jonathan said, joining Bob in applause.

Kate hung in the background.

The riders both got off the Harley with their duffle bags and took a big bow. Mitch headed toward them, and everyone else followed, "You two had this planned!? Whose...?"

"It's ours...mine and my husband's. I talked Graham into riding with me! I'm usually the one on the back seat. I could get used to driving!"

"Ride of my life!" Graham said, punching his arm up in the air.

"Motorcycle Mama!" Jonathan said. "You been keepin' secrets, girl!"

Leslie gave him a smile and a little shrug as the group headed back toward the cabin.

"I always assumed you owned a pair of chaps, but I never imagined they served any *utilitarian* purpose," Stephen chided Graham, a bit more good-naturedly than usual.

"You just never can tell about these things..." Graham said out of the corner of his mouth with a sly grin, not giving away too much.

Back on the porch, the mood was suddenly much lighter. Mitch asked everyone to stand in a circle. Evening was just beginning to fall, and he realized that they would be able to watch the sunset while together making the dinner that Graham had all planned out. Before they went inside, Mitch thanked them for coming, saying, "Each one of you is remarkable, unique, and irreplaceable. I want you to know how much I value you...and you and you and you..." he said, looking around the circle. "Now let's eat! Then we'll get down to some basics."

"This is the last time," Mitch said, pushing away his dessert plate and taking a sip of coffee, "that you'll see me at the head of the table—literally or figuratively—this weekend. Our time here will not be spent with me trying to show the rest of you the way. That method hasn't worked so well in the past...as we all know." Leslie flashed him the ever-supportive smile. "Our time here will be spent creating the way together.

"In preparation for tomorrow's activities, I'd like to present you with six words. We won't discuss them formally now. Everyone just grab one of those pieces of paper from the center of the table and write them down. I ask that you spend some time considering what they mean to you. Maybe even do some free writing, some journaling, some doodling, some talking amongst yourselves...Whatever comes to you."

Mitch said the words one by one: **trust, talent, truth, team, touchstones, transformation**. Glances were exchanged, but no one said anything. "We'll get up tomorrow, make breakfast, have an hour or so to go hiking or whatever...and then we'll convene at 10am."

Elizabeth looked around the table and finally spoke up. "So, what exactly are we doing for the next two and a half days?"

"We, my friends, are taking responsibility for discussing our passions...and then creating ourselves, our company and a better world out of a whirlwind of order and chaos. Details to follow. Cheers," he said lifting his coffee cup, pardoning himself from the table and wishing he'd had a hidden camera running to capture the range of expressions. Graham caught Kate's eye with a knowing grin. Stephen was more intrigued than he cared to let on. Charles looked like he was lost in the second act of a Greek tragedy. Maureen asked Leslie for an aspirin and headed to bed.

The next morning, with everyone but Kate seated in a circle on the large living room rug, Mitch placed large sheets of butcher paper and colored pens in the center. "It seems we all agree that this is a beautiful spot, but I'm sure some of you are wondering why we didn't just book some hotel and conference center in the city. Well, I'll tell you why." Mitch explained his childhood creativity connection with being near water. "It's taken over six months of coaching with Kate," he said, acknowledging where she was seated at the back of the room, "for me to regain that part of myself. I wanted to share it all with you this weekend...and tap into your creative sides, as well."

He spilled his guts over their last coaching session. The fire, the water...and everything they represented for him. He also explained how his ongoing repetition of the T-words through his coaching process had brought both him and Kate to the conclusion that they should represent the core values on which the new and improved Global Trade Management should be built. "But I want your input on them...what they mean to you...and what you feel they should mean to our employees and our customers. Our core values are and will always be a give and take, an ebb and flow...like water...ever-changing, unstoppable, dynamic!"

"Well, I think that..." Leslie started to say.

Mitch asked her to wait, saying that they were about to engage in a forum to discuss the core values and much, much more. "How many of you are familiar with the concept of Open Space Technology?" Graham and Leslie raised their hands; Elizabeth started to but hesitated. "Well, allow me..." he continued, saying that Kate had enlightened him on the subject, and he liked the idea. He explained that organizational consultant Harrison Owen created Open Space Technology in the mid 1980's when he realized that people attending his conferences loved the coffee breaks better than the formal presentations and sessions. "Hmm...I guess some things are universal and timeless--recess...coffee breaks...go figure!" Mitch said, getting laughs all around. "Anyway, Owen combined that insight with his experience of life in an African village—very open and free-flowing—to create a totally new form of conferencing.

"This weekend, no one leads and no one follows. You are all free to conduct your own mini-workshops on any topic of your choice. Whoever feels moved to do so, take a piece of paper from the center, write down your topic and announce it to the group." Everyone sat silently looking at one another. Mitch was loving this process, and he knew that Kate was taking mental notes in the background. "Alright, then!" He grabbed a paper and wrote in blue ink **Core Values**. "That is the subject of my workshop. Next, please!"

Leslie was suddenly giddy. She practically pounced on the paper and wrote in very fancy green letters, ***Attracting and Maintaining Top Talent***. Graham started to reach for paper but held back. Bob stepped up, apparently to Maureen's chagrin, and wrote in brown, **Attracting and Maintaining New Accounts.** Jonathan wrote one word, **Offsites!** with every letter in a different color. Elizabeth finally joined in, writing **Design** in bright orange.

Mitch was impressed; he hadn't counted on so much participation. "Wow... well, we've got five topics and eight people. We'll all circulate! I ask one thing. Don't go through the motions. Go to the subjects you feel passionately about or don't go at all. As you do, I ask that you bear in mind this OST principle. It's called The Law of Two Feet: *If you find yourself in a situation where you aren't learning or contributing, go somewhere else.* Take it literally or take it as a metaphor for moving to an untapped space in your mind. But take it...and have fun with it! Now, isn't this better than putting a slide in the break room?" he concluded with a laugh, making a reference to his own response to the 360-feedback. Kate shot him a wink and a smile from across the room. "Now go forth and multiply...your ideas, that is!"

Everyone posted their papers in different spots and then milled around a bit. Jonathan got lots of traffic right off the bat, with everyone throwing in ideas for future offsites. He told Leslie that he'd go with any of her ideas...as long as she took him for a ride on the Harley.

Mitch was busy brainstorming words and the core values when Bob joined him, followed by Maureen and Charles. The two of them seemed to be following their Chairman's lead. Without a word, Bob took the pen out of Mitch's hand and wrote something under each T-word. Under **Trust**...integrity. Under **Team**...best and brightest. Under **Truth**...authentic leadership. Under **Team**...values. Under **Touchstones**...excellence. Under **Transformation**...positive change. "These words reflect the core values you've created, Mitchell. And this company's core values are a direct reflection of its CEO. I mean that. I had no idea what we were in for when you took my suggestion and found a coach. You've exceeded my expectations."

Mitch could hardly speak. "Thank you, Bob."

"No, thank you," he said, shaking his hand and placing a big, reassuring hand on Mitch's arm before moving on to the next station, his smiling, nodding cohorts in tow.

Graham chose to put most of his creative effort into the food. Everyone chipped in and either helped prepare lunch or cleaned up afterward. Then they were off to the afternoon session.

They each made the rounds, brainstorming, discussing and jotting down key words at each of the stations. Mitch was caught up in the inspiration he felt with everyone's contribution to his list and was freewriting on his third piece of butcher paper. When he realized that the room had grown suddenly quiet, he turned around and realized why. The group was huddled around Elizabeth. He rushed over, fearing something might be wrong.

"Check it out," Jonathan said as Mitch peeked over his shoulder. He felt his eyes grow wide. She was painting, in bold, vivid colors, her vision of what Global's redesigned foyer, lobby and front office should look like. Open, airy, inviting. At the center of the room was a self-contained fountain that looked more like a waterfall.

In a split second, Mitch realized that it was the exact same style as the paintings in her office. Jonathan stepped back and everyone else followed his lead, making room for Mitch, who reached out, as if to touch the beautiful picture.

"Elizabeth...I never realized..."

"You never asked," she said. "But then again, I s'pose I never shared much, either. So, this Open Space Technology, if it's partially inspired by the dynamics of an African village, then I guess you could say it's in my blood. And I'm thinking..." she said as she continued to paint, "that the whole concept can be reflected in how we design and decorate the new space."

"I'm all ears," Mitch said. And he meant it.

That evening before the dinner break, Kate approached Mitch's station. "I think I'm gonna head back home," she said.

"What? We're just getting started!"

She'd overheard Bob's comments to him earlier in the day. "No, you're not. You're well underway. You've got your team back, Mitch. It's not my place to participate here, anyway. I just wanted to observe, to see you in your element. I'd say...you are fully engaged."

By the end of the second night, each of the topics had been expanded greatly. Seated in a circle again, everyone shared the sum of knowledge and insights that the group had contributed to their original idea. Mitch was proud to read Global's Core Values:

As a living, breathing organization, Global Trade will be dedicated to building:

Trust: our clients, employees, board, stakeholders and the public will know without a shadow of a doubt that this company is built on the foundation of integrity, strength and credibility.

Talent: a team of people who are the best and brightest in the field. They will be attracted and trained on the basis of building leaders for the future. Our clients will also know that it is our goal to support them in building substantial income and streamlining their trading processes so that they can also attract and retain top talent.

Truth: we will speak from a place of truth...not just from a place that is honest but from a place that honors the authentic life and leadership style of each employee, client and stakeholder we serve. We will be training our employees to lead from a place of truth....a place which allows their talents and strengths to guide the work they do.

Team: we are not merely a group thrown together for the sake of working for Global; we are a highly talented collection of men and women who are working together in the direction of living the values, vision and mission of Global. Collaboration and the mastermind process will be tapped daily to help fulfill this living, breathing value.

Touchstones: by raising our own bar, we will be developing a standard of excellence that will be used to test the excellence and genuineness of our employees, clients, competitors and all stakeholders.

Transformation: by calling forth the creativity, talent, collaboration, trust and authentic leadership style of each stakeholder we serve, Global will create positive change and a huge impact in our corporate community, local community of Washington D.C. and the world. We will be creating a foundation that will donate scholarships and grants to people and organizations whose work lines up with our core values and is creating transformation.

Bob was the first to rise, starting a complete standing ovation. Mitch quickly stood, too, reminding everyone that they were clapping for themselves, as well. "I didn't create our core values. We did!" With that, they were off to celebrate with a grand finale of bonfire and s'mores...Graham's idea, of course.

As they all sat around, Mitch realized how much he'd gotten used to seeing everyone so casual and relaxed. Everyone but Stephen, who had just never quite gotten into the groove of the weekend. Sitting there on a log all night, even with his sleeves rolled up, he was looked so out of place in his Dockers and button up shirt. Mitch couldn't resist the question on his mind.

"So, Stephen, suppose you had started a topic for the weekend. What would it have been?"

"Aw, Mitch. You know me. I'm just the cold, hard facts. The numbers guy."

Mitch remembered the day of the fire and knew better. "Nah. C'mon my friend. I'm not buyin' that."

Stephen was quiet for a moment. He stared into the fire and through it, his elbows on his knees. "Well, like they say, you can take the boy outta of the blue-blood, but you can't take the blue-blood outta the boy."

Mitch was used to hearing such things from him with a tone of arrogance. This time it sounded more like candor or maybe even a little grief.

"Hey, wait here," Stephen said, suddenly jumping up and running to get something out of the trunk of his car. He came back with a gym bag in his hand. Out of it, he pulled something completely unexpected. The light of the fire revealed what remained of Mitch's Pee Chee folder—his script and grad school application still inside. The whole top right corner of each of them was burned away.

"I, uh...I thought you might want these. Found 'em last week in the bins of unclaimed items leftover from the fire."

Mitch hesitated for a moment. Of all the things that could have gone through his mind, it struck him how strange it was to see them in someone else's hands.

"Um...thank you. I uh..." It was then that he realized he'd completely forgotten about them. He reached for them and took them from Stephen.

"Well, I'm gonna head in." Stephen turned to walk away but hesitated. "Mitch...thanks. I just wanna say thanks."

Mitch nodded and smiled as he watched Stephen walk away. He wondered if, in the long run, Stephen would choose to stay or to go. And if he left, where would he go, and would he find his way? Then he realized that he felt a little sad for the first time all weekend.

He laid the brittle folder on his knees and opened it carefully. Feeling unaffected by knowing that it had been gone made him feel a strange but certain lightness. He saw the reflection of the flames as they seemed to dance to the rhythm of the water lapping on the shore just feet from him. He tossed the folder into the fire and smiled as its light grew brighter.

The next morning when he awoke, he knew they'd all be having one last break-fast together and maybe a little hike before heading home. When he opened the bedroom door, there was something at his feet. It was the picture that Elizabeth had painted, along with six smooth river rocks and a note. *I want you to have this picture. It's all of ours, really, but I want you to have it because you inspired me to create it. I also want you to have these stones. I went for a hike early this morning to where the river feeds the lake. There is one stone for each of us and one for the Board...smoothed by the current...ever-changing, unstoppable, dynamic...just like you said. Touchstones. We are all touchstones, Mitch.*

Mitch looked at the picture again and noticed that there were six touchstones placed in the wall over which the waterfall flowed. He heard a car outside and walked to the window to see Elizabeth headed up the road toward home.

Redesigning

Today, as the leader of your company, organization, community, family or congre-gation, you have the opportunity to redesign your company, your organization, your community or your life. With the power of technology and the support of the bright, talented people in your network of support, you have the chance to dream bigger than you ever have in world history and to make that dream become a reality.

In Chapter 21, Mitch invites his team to a retreat to join him in taking responsi-bility for discussing their vision for the future of Global. As the CEO of Global, Mitch came to the retreat with a basic dream in mind...a vision of what he wanted both his life and his organization to look like in the future, and he did not take this on alone. He invited his team to look within to explore what they most deeply cared about as individuals, as a team and as a living, breathing, dynamic organiza-tion. As a result, in this one weekend, the Global team begins to design a radically creative transformation that ignites a new passion in the organization.

Coaching Questions:

As you consider redesigning your company, organization, community or congregation, take the time to answer the following questions:

- What is a big dream that you had ages ago that you have given up on? What is it that caused you to give up on that big dream?

- What is your **big** dream for the future of your organization or life? What does it look like and feel like? Be as descriptive as possible, and don't hold back as you dream.

- What steps will you take, starting today, to move in the direction of making your big dream into a reality for your organization, community, family, company or congregation? Brainstorm on paper at least 100 strategies you can use to make your dream come alive.

- How will you get your team, members, congregation or community leaders truly excited about your dream and to participate in helping you stretch out your dream so that it becomes a source of inspiration for others?

- Once your big dream is realized, what transformation will happen in others and the world around you? Think both locally and globally as you answer this question.

BONUS: As a way to support you in making your big dream a reality, Michael E. Gerber, NY Times best-selling author of the *The E-Myth Revisited* and *Awakening the Entrepreneur Within: How Ordinary People Can Create Extraordinary Companies* and creator of "In the Dreaming Room," will provide *Edge* readers with multiple teleconferences where readers can come dream with Michael and have their leadership world turned upside down! For more information, visit http://www.Edge-Book.com/bonus.

TWENTY TWO | Standing Up

"**Y**ou're choked up!" Mitch said, catching Graham off guard for a change, as they stood there together and looked around the grand foyer of the office on the big day.

"Nah...I'm, I'm fine," he answered, avoiding eye contact.

"You can't fool me..." Mitch wasn't about to let up.

"I guess I just realize now—looking around at the physical proof of the changes that all of us and this company have gone through and have yet to go through—that while every cell in my body was pulling for you, *wanted* to believe in you...there was a small part of me that wasn't sure you'd go the distance, Mitch. I'm embarrassed to admit that, but it's true." He looked down for a moment and then straight into Mitch's eyes. "And you did it. Nay-sayers be damned, you did it."

Mitch didn't know what to say, so he said nothing at first. "I owe a lot of it to you, my friend. I guess I should thank you for calling me out on my bullshit. You and Kate have a lot in common that way. In fact, I think you two were actually separated at birth."

"Well, speak of the devil!" Graham said as Kate walked through the front doors.

Several steps inside, she stopped with her eyes wide and her mouth agape. After scanning the unrecognizable room, she crossed one arm over her chest and put the opposite hand over her mouth.

"Mitch..." was all she could manage. "I expected great things, but..."

One or two smartass remarks came to mind, but Mitch chose just to smile instead and take in the moment. Besides, with the unveiling and grand re-opening party that evening, he was trying to pace himself.

"Shall we, m'lady?" Graham said, offering his arm. Without a word, Kate stepped forward and draped her wrist over his arm. Looking skyward, the three of them walked slowly past a couple of open, circular seating areas to the center of the room. The expanse of the high windowed ceiling with wood and steel beams was still a bit breathtaking to Mitch, too. They stopped in front of the self-contained waterfall in the center of the room.

"The six touchstones you mentioned," Kate finally said, putting her hand in the water to actually touch one of them, placed ever so subtly in the formation.

The almost countless conversations they'd had over the last year or so ran through Mitch's head in a matter of a few seconds. He noticed a tear at the corner of one of Kate's eyes and knew that she was probably taking in the fruition of their work together, too. Graham instinctively patted her on the shoulder, gave Mitch a wink and headed off to leave them to their business.

"As you know, I'm seldom speechless. I'm just...so impressed by what you— you and your team—have created here, Mitch." She looked to the brick and wood beam-accented walls beyond the waterfall. Slightly to the right were bright, vivid poster size photos of team members engaged in working with clients, a few taken in the old office, many already in the new office and some in international locations. Interspersed with those were more obvious touchstones, each one with one of the

T-words etched into them. In the center of it all were their complete core values, framed and displayed on tapestry for the world to see. To the left, behind the reception desk, was an international map with lighted pin-dots of locations of clients. To the side of the map was an actual list of clients...with room for plenty more.

As they turned to enter the actual office space, Kate noticed the picture. There at the top of the arch hung Elizabeth's painting, her conception of what the front office should be. Kate smiled. "Mitch, what I can already tell you about this new office is that it just simply rings true. I know from our conversations that you all worked very closely with the designer...and it shows. It's not something that someone came in and created from the outside in. It feels organic. It truly reflects not just where you are, but where you've been and where you want to go. No one needs to know the details of your path to appreciate the obvious *authenticity* of your path. It's something that you can *feel* from the moment you open the door."

With that vote of confidence, they headed off to see the workspaces, and Mitch explained what a good sounding board Anna had been in the architectural design process, too. Of course, Global hadn't used her firm, but pillow talk about the stresses and concerns of the process had been invaluable to him...and a nice new common ground that they'd forged.

The new hallway was wide and airy, a far cry from the narrow-walled, dark wood-grain of the past. Before they knew it, they were in a common area with warm orange and beige walls, wood accents and circular seating areas; all of the chairs and couches were low to the ground and comfy looking. In contrast were, again, the high ceilings with windowed areas. "The combination to keep us grounded and remind us to soar," Mitch said, quoting Elizabeth and giving her credit for the idea. Off to one side was a ream of butcher paper on a roller with a jar of colored pens on the side...reminiscent of the brainstorming they'd done during the offsite.

"Nice touch!" Kate said, and Mitch remarked that they planned to have many an OST style session.

Surrounding the area were the workspaces, executives on one side, up a few stairs, and other departments scattered around the rest of the perimeter. More photos like those in the foyer were scattered around the walls. Mitch guided Kate around one corner to the offices *sans* doors to see Jonathan tapping away at his laptop while seated in the beanbag chair. He smiled and leapt up to give her a hug.

"Looks like the beanbag is the lone surviving piece of furniture from the old office!" Kate said with a smile.

"Yeah, I started something, as you'll see..." he said with a wink.

Jonathan's eclectic taste was reflected in the theater posters, photos of his hiking trips, and various Mac enthusiast paraphernalia. There was even a guitar perched on a stand in one corner "...for inspiration," he told Kate.

The rest of the individual offices had the same personal touches that made the entire office and the work they created there feel genuine, like an extension of the lives of the Board, the executive team and the employees...not just an objective, removed place of work.

After her grand entrance at the offsite, Leslie finally had the guts to display several pictures of her and her husband's Harley road-trips along with, naturally, an ever-expanding veritable mural of their tow-headed five-year old daughter. And a bright red beanbag chair.

Graham's office boasted Salvador Dali prints and classic photos, paintings, and pop-culture representations of fine food and wine. And a bright multi-colored bean bag chair, of course.

Elizabeth's display of her paintings had expanded a bit, and obviously with pride, now that her secret was out. The bright, urban, and frequently ethnic themes were everywhere on the walls. In one corner next to a low end table with a sketchpad and colored pencils...a bright orange beanbag.

Stephen's office was a bit of an anachronism, squeezed into a 21st century work-space. He did his best, decorating the walls with photos of urban night scenes. He'd chosen some dark accents to tone down the bright hues that surrounded him, most notably the mahogany tabletop clock on the sideboard handed down by his grandfather. In the corner was a dark blue obligatory beanbag.

Bob's office was a brilliant blend of old meets new. The wingback chairs, too, had survived, and actually blended well with the combination of modern leather couch and plush, tan pillow back couch and light wood tables and desk. Bob drew the line at the beanbag chair idea, but did agree to another couple of cushiony chairs and circular arrangement.

As they moseyed their way to the end of the similarly designed remaining departments and meeting rooms, Mitch offered Kate some coffee, picking up the pace a bit. "Get a load of this!" he said, ushering her into the kitchen and lounge area. Stainless steel, wood accents, brick. Warm but modern and inviting. Again, there were a couple of circular seating areas. He adeptly whipped up a couple of cappuccinos for them with the new espresso machine. Kate hadn't stopped smil-ing yet, he thought. With the first sip, Mitch decided that it was the best cappuc-cino he'd ever tasted. Not that it really was, but *perception is everything*, he reminded himself, and it seemed to him that he was on a roll.

"And now..." he said, as he ushered her into his also doorless office with a sweep of his arm. *You've come a long way, baby*, he told himself as his coach surveyed the space with obvious admiration.

"Love the poster!" she said, indicating the vintage *Laugh Factory* flier advertising a John Candy performance back in the day. Surrounding it were other film and comedy posters. On the opposite wall were pictures of his family, most notably of their recent vacation together. Mitch thought that Kate seemed to take special note of the autographed Orson Welles photo, never knowing, of course, that Gra-ham had clued her in months before. Next to it sat the group photo of everyone at the offsite.

"Well, well," she said. "What a journey this has been, Mitch...and will continue to be. Everything here is new...but old at the same time, you know...an evolution, of sorts. It's a nice feeling. All of these physical changes in the office are brilliant. But what's most impressive is that it's all a reflection of you...of the changes in you and your team."

"Well, thank you. And as angry and scared as I was, thank goodness for the fire, I guess."

"No...the fire was just an added impetus. I say this not as your coach any longer, but as your friend. You would've made these changes without the fire, Mitch. It may have taken a bit longer, but you would've gotten there. I know it now."

He pondered that idea for a moment. "Yes," he said, looking directly at her. "You're right. I would have made these changes no matter what. In the end, I wouldn't have settled for anything less." They raised their cappuccinos in a toast.

A few hours later, the caterers had everything laid out for the reception, and people were starting to assemble for the grand unveiling. The media was buzzing around. Mitch was pacing a bit in his office when Anna and the boys arrived. She stood beaming in the doorway for a moment before he looked up and saw her. They embraced firmly, and he held her when she went to pull away.

"I'm so glad you're here," he whispered.

"Wouldn't have missed it for the world," she said, as she relaxed back into his arms and Kyle and Daniel wrestled for a beanbag chair.

Thirty minutes later, the CEO found himself standing in front of several hundred people. His team, the Board, and his family were in the front row. Kate sat in back but in clear view.

Mitch welcomed everyone and, as part of the plan, with mock, humorous disgust, asked a couple of the men to remove the archaic podium from the platform before he began. Out of the corner of his eye, he saw Graham laugh and the team exchange glances. He thanked everyone for coming and for express- ing their consistent support for Global Trade Management. He explained that he wanted to talk about the obvious physical changes in the company, but even more so, wanted to talk about what the changes represented: their intentions to do life-changing, world-improving work beyond the confines of their walls and their typical scope; their plans for scholarships and programs yet unforeseen; their focus on relationships within and without the walls of the building itself; and their core values and how they had arrived at them.

"Before we go there, though," Mitch said with a droll swagger as his demeanor changed. He took off his jacket and glasses, rolled up his sleeves, loosened his tie and took a swig from his water bottle. "I want to paint you all a little picture. I used to know this CEO...Now before you get too impressed, I'm not talking about a Chief Executive Officer. Oh, don't get me wrong, that *used to be* his title. But with time, people started to think of him more as the...**Celibate Egotistical Opiate**...because he was so damned self-absorbed and boring that he alienated everybody or put them to sleep!" Mitch said it all with gusto, laughing at himself.

Anna stared wide-eyed at the husband who had been full of one surprise after another lately. Graham let out a hoot that started a round of applause.

"When he was asked to spearhead the redesign of the office...ay...what a disaster! Oh, you thought he'd hire a designer? Oh no! Not this guy. He could do everything all by himself! One-man band and solo act, all in one. His conde- scending rise to the challenge of providing more opportunities for his team and employees to have more fun at work?...putting a slide in the break room! A *slide?* Yes, a slide. Oh, but the renovation of which he was most proud?...IV centers in every office. Yep! Everyone had their own portable IV. You know those wheeled, stand-up drip bag stands that you can conveniently haul around with you. Not for sedatives, though...no...no. No, the IV's allowed everyone to mainline coffee for 8-hours a day to combat the suffocating pall of **boredom** that threatened to take out the entire staff!

"Yeah...now most of you don't know this, but I'm actually a famous retired film director. You thought I'd always been a day-job guy...*au contraire. Dawn of the Dead?*...yeah, that was mine. I made that. When they were looking for extras, I saved 'em a fortune. They didn't even have to hire actors! The mall scene...yeah, that was my CEO friend and his staff. Every day, after a couple hours in the office, they all entered in a zombie-state anyway, so we just corralled 'em, hauled 'em off to the mall and let 'em wander. Brilliant!"

There was not a wandering eye in the house. Everyone laughed with each other and with Mitch. Even the seemingly unreachable Maureen had taken an evening away from the country club and had a smile on her face. Although the volume of the room roared, as Mitch looked directly into the faces and the cameras, he was swept away and heard nothing, not the flicker of an 8mm camera, not the sound of water over stones, not even the sound of his own voice. It was the silence of countless possibilities spread before him just as a blank white canvas was the combination of all colors. It terrified and inspired him, and he suddenly recognized what authenticity felt like. He forced himself back to the present, opened his mouth, and the words came out.

"Hey, anyone know the new A-word? Come on...some guesses..." Mitch was off and running in his first stand-up/improv routine. He was no prime-time comic, but he did have the entire room in smiles and laughs, with even the camera operators peeking around their equipment.

At the end of his routine and the rest of his speech, while the crowd applauded, he looked up to see Kate holding up her wine glass in a toast to him. He nodded and bowed a couple of times, and when he looked back, her chair was empty. He felt both sad and exhilarated, knowing that the journey hadn't ended; it had simply taken a new direction. With Kate, he knew he'd created the tools he needed to intentionally carve a path he could call his own with every passing day. Raising his own glass in a toast in her direction, he thanked her under his breath.

He came down from the platform and spent the rest of the evening engaged in conversations with the people who would help him to hone and define and value every step he took from that point forward.

Standing Up

Standing up for what you believe in. Standing alone in times of uncertainty. Living authentically. Being courageous. Great leaders must take these steps in order to make a positive impact on their companies, families, communities, congregations and organizations. While it may sound simple in theory, living the life of a leader in deed—day in and day out—takes courage and guts.

In this closing chapter, Mitchell James stands up and reveals his authentic self to everybody present: his team, his employees, the Board, his friends, his family and the public at large via the media. I believe that, in this day and age, we need much more of this kind of leadership. Leaders, in all kinds of settings, need to stand up and think and play bigger about who they are and what they can give to the world.

Coaching Questions:

- What do you care about deeply enough to take a stand for it, knowing that you may be criticized by your followers in the process?

- On a scale of 1-10, how willing are you to be comfortable with discomfort? If you're uncomfortable with discomfort, what causes that current discomfort?

- What are the needs of your community, family, company or organization? How willing are you to put their needs ahead of your own in order to grow as a person?

- To which do you have a stronger commitment? Your big goal or dream or your current way of doing things? If you have a stronger commitment to your current thoughts and actions, what are you afraid will happen if you really commit yourself to fulfilling your big goal or dream?

- If you had to stand up today and speak from the heart about who you are and what you truly believe in, what would you say?

- What steps will you take, starting today, to play a much bigger game in life?

BONUS: In order to support you in taking a stand for what you believe in and in playing a much bigger game in life, Michael Port, best selling author and Founder of the *Think Big Revolution,* has opened a private section of our website to allow you, our readers of *Edge,* the opportunity to start your own Think Big Revolution for your company, community, organization, congregation, school or family. For more information, visit http://www.Edge-Book.com/bonus.

BONUS RECAP:

BONUS: As a way to support you in beginning to work through your **Fear**, Roger Dewitt of Coaching NYC Inc. has provided an audio, workbook and guided imagery for readers of *Edge*. For more information, visit http://www.Edge-Book.com/bonus.

BONUS: As a way to support you in beginning to address the topic of **Avoidance**, Kimberly George, author of *Coaching Into Greatness* has designed the EDGE Abundance Assessment. Specifically designed for leaders of today, this cutting edge assessment will raise your awareness around your current level of avoidance and resistance and will provide you with practical steps that can move anyone past their avoidance to embrace the Abundance Aptitudes of Self-Worth, Empathy, Self-Expression, Surrender, Actualization, Significance and Inquiry. The assessment is available online through this link: http://www.Edge-Book.com/bonus.

BONUS: We invite you, as a reader of *Edge*, to start **Digging** into your personal manifesto. As a way to get you started, Andy Wibbels, author of *BLOG Wild!* has opened a private blog area for you to begin this process: http://www.Edge-book.com/bonus. As you are writing, answer the following coaching questions.

BONUS: In order to support you in answering these and other questions pertaining to the subject of being **Blindsided**, Carol Dickson Carr, President of Managing Personal Resources, has provided readers of *Edge* with a **Facing Challenges** audio and action guide. To gain access to this guide, please visit http://www.Edge-book.com/bonus.

BONUS: In an effort to assist you in **Taking Command**, Writers of the Round Table Inc., is inviting *Edge* readers to participate in a teleclass called *Taking Command: How to determine your Core Values and use them to raise your stakes!* For more information, visit http://www.Edge-Book.com/bonus.

BONUS: As a way to support you in **Redesigning** your big dream, Michael E. Gerber, NY Times best-selling author of the *The E-Myth Revisited* and *Awakening the Entrepreneur Within: How Ordinary People Can Create Extraordinary Companies* and creator of "In the Dreaming Room," will provide *Edge* readers with multiple tele-conferences where readers can come dream with Michael and have their leadership world turned upside down! For more information, visit http://www.Edge-Book.com/bonus.

BONUS: In order to support you in **Standing Up** for what you believe in and in playing a much bigger game in life, Michael Port, best selling author and Founder of the *Think Big Revolution,* has opened a private section of our website to allow you, our readers of *Edge,* the opportunity to start your own Think Big Revolution for your company, community, organization, congregation, school or family. For more information, visit http://www.Edge-Book.com/bonus.

Bea Fields

Bea Fields is the President of Bea Fields Companies, Inc. and the Founder of Five Star Leader Coaching and Training, a leadership consulting firm currently serving over 800 clients world-wide.

Her first book, co-authored with Scott Wilder, Jim Bunch and Rob Newbold, *Millennial Leaders: Success Stories From Today's Most Brilliant Generation Y Leaders* is now on sale through Barnes & Noble and Amazon. The new book explores and analyzes Generation Y—the young adults currently between the ages of 18 and 30—from a socio-economic standpoint. The book highlights 25 members of this generation who have already made a name for themselves, and provides crucial insights for business and political leaders seeking to tap into this demographic.

Fields' educational background includes a bachelor's degree from The University of Alabama, and a certificate degree in Leadership Coaching from Georgetown University in Washington, DC. She holds several important certifications which include The International Coach Federation's Professional Certified Coach (PCC) designation and the Guerrilla Marketing coach certification. She received the Thomas Leonard Award in 2006, which is an honor bestowed on a coach who has exhibited mastery in the profession of coaching.

Bea Fields Companies, Inc. has had great success in using a variety of leadership and business development programs to assist clients in the areas of leadership and team development, strategic planning, business development, strategic alliance development, training and event development, creative writing, leadership branding, and public speaking.

In addition to her consulting work, Fields maintains an active role in her community. She has served on the Board of Visitors for The University of North Carolina's Children's Hospital, and the board of directors for The Sandhills Children's Center in Southern Pines, North Carolina. She has also served as a director for The FirstHealth Hospice Foundation in Pinehurst, North Carolina, and The Episcopal Day School in Southern Pines, North Carolina. She is the Chairman Elect for the Board of Directors of the Moore County Chamber of Commerce.

Fields lives in Southern Pines, NC with her husband, Mike. She is the mother of three: Ann Fields, Sophomore at Duke University, Katie Fields, Sophomore at Wofford College and Jack Fields, who is a Senior at Pine Crest High School and will be attending and playing golf for the University of North Carolina starting in August 2008.

Corey Blake

With more than a dozen national commercial campaigns including Mountain Dew, Pepsi, McDonalds, Wrigley's, Hasbro, and Mitsubishi under his belt and appearances on popular T.V. shows like The Shield, Buffy the Vampire Slayer, Diagnosis Murder, VIP, and Fastlane, Corey Blake put an end to his lucrative commercial and television acting career to pursue his passion for writing. In 2000, he founded Elevation 9000 Films and went on to spearhead the original Elevation 9000 Film Lab that eventually inspired the motion picture production company LA Film Lab Entertainment and Writers of the Round Table Inc.

For the past eight years, Corey Blake has played a key role in the development of more than three hundred screenplays and manuscripts. He has won nine festival awards for his work in entertainment and contributed articles to nearly three dozen industry publications including Script Magazine, Writer Magazine (cover article), and the Los Angeles Journal. Corey Blake's work as a writer and development producer has been featured on Fox News and in articles in Backstage West, MovieMaker Magazine, Hollywood Scriptwriter Magazine and Dance Magazine. He speaks around the country on various topics related to writing and publishing.

Corey's name is attached as the author or co-author to twelve projects for release in 2008 and 2009 including fiction, non-fiction and screenplays. In addition to *Edge! A Leadership Story*, Corey told Robert Renteria's *From the Barrio to the Board Room* (Writers of the Round Table Press, February 2008), and is co-author with Angelica Harris on *Excalibur Reclaims Her King* (Writers of the Round Table Press, 2009)

Corey is proudly married to Dr. Dawn Blake, a Psychologist. They make their home in the suburbs of Chicago with their precocious pup, Daisy.

Eva Silva Travers

With roots in both print and broadcast media, Eva Silva Travers is a writer with a broad scope of experience. In the corporate world, she has enjoyed success as a writer, producer and digital editor for several production companies and as a radio newscaster/announcer. Her real passion, though, thrives in the creative world. Eva has been involved with the creation of numerous scripts, screenplays and treatments for major production companies and sold a screenplay to internationally recognized Graz Entertainment. She earned an Associate of Arts Degree in Radio and Television and a Bachelor of Arts in Literature and Writing Studies and won a Student Emmy Award for a documentary on teenage alcoholism while in college. As Director of All Things Creative for Writers of the Round Table, she enjoys the constant momentum and synergy of engaging clients and writers in the creation of inspiring manuscripts. She speaks and facilitates workshops in schools and public forums on the creation of engaging characters and successful manuscripts. She is an active member of the Los Angeles Writers Group.

As time allows, Eva also enjoys writing freelance restaurant and pop-culture reviews, having been published in numerous periodicals. She has also acted, modeled and done voice-over work part-time for nearly thirty years and still completes occasional assignments. She lives in Los Angeles and San Diego with her two wonderfully rambunctious sons and her talented husband, drummer and Vaultmeister for the Zappa Family Trust, Joe Travers.

Printed in the United Kingdom by
Lightning Source UK Ltd., Milton Keynes
142581UK00001B/58/P